Adam Mickiewicz

BALLADS AND ROMANCES

GLAGOSLAV PUBLICATIONS

BALLADS AND ROMANCES

by Adam Mickiewicz

Translated from the Polish and introduced by
Charles S. Kraszewski

This publication is generously supported
by the Polish Cultural Institute in London.

Proofreading by Richard Coombes

Publishers
Maxim Hodak & Max Mendor

Introduction and English translation © 2022, Charles S. Kraszewski
Cover art and illustration on page 4 © 2022, Max Mendor
© 2022, Glagoslav Publications

Book cover and interior book design by Max Mendor

www.glagoslav.com

ISBN: 978-1-80484-000-9

Published by Glagoslav Publications in September 2022.
A catalogue record for this book is available from the British Library.

This book is in copyright. No part of this publication may be reproduced, stored in a retrieval system or transmitted in any form or by any means without the prior permission in writing of the publisher, nor be otherwise circulated in any form of binding or cover other than that in which it is published without a similar condition, including this condition, being imposed on the subsequent purchaser.

Adam Mickiewicz

BALLADS AND ROMANCES

Translated from the Polish
and introduced by Charles S. Kraszewski

GLAGOSLAV PUBLICATIONS

Adam Mickiewicz

1798 – 1855

Contents

INTRODUCTION: DEAR MARYLA. DEAR YOU. ON THE UNIVERSAL APPLICATION OF MICKIEWICZ'S *BALLADS AND ROMANCES* 7

FROM *BALLADS AND ROMANCES* (WILNO, 1822)

1. THE PRIMROSE 48
2. ROMANTICISM 50
3. ŚWITEŹ 53
4. THE ŚWITEZIANKA 60
5. THE LITTLE FISH 66
6. PAPA'S RETURN 71
7. MARYLA'S MOUND 74
8. TO MY FRIENDS 78
9. THIS I LIKE 80
10. THE GLOVE 85
11. MRS TWARDOWSKA 87
12. TUKAJ OR TESTS OF FRIENDSHIP 92
13. THE LILIES 101
14. THE MINSTREL 112

POEMS ADDED TO *BALLADS AND ROMANCES* (LEIPZIG, 1852)

15. THE LURKERS 120
16. THE ESCAPE 122
17. THE THREE BUDRYSES 128
18. THE RENEGADE 130

BIBLIOGRAPHY 132

ABOUT THE AUTHOR 134
ABOUT THE TRANSLATOR 135

TO JAN CZECZOT
TOMASZ ZAN
JÓZEF JEŻOWSKI
AND
FRANCISZEK MALEWSKI
IN REMEMBRANCE OF THE JOYOUS TIMES
OF OUR YOUTH, WHICH WE EXPERIENCED TOGETHER

THIS COLLECTION IS DEDICATED

ADAM MICKIEWICZ

INTRODUCTION

Dear Maryla. Dear You.
On the Universal Application of Mickiewicz's
Ballads and Romances

Charles S. Kraszewski

I don't know whether Adam Mickiewicz ever found himself in Slovakia. I do know that, after extricating himself from Russian interior banishment in 1829, he travelled west, through Berlin and Dresden, and visited Prague on his way to Italy.[1] But that was probably as close as he got to the land I'm sitting in right now, writing these words. His influence on Slovak poetry during the key years when the modern national consciousness was forming in fevered opposition to the Magyarising policies of the Kingdom of Hungary is unquestionable, to mention just Ľudovit Štúr's *Starý a nový věk Slovakův* [The Slovaks, in Ancient Days and Now, 1841],[2] conceived under the indubitable influence of Mickiewicz's quasi-Biblical *Księgi narodu polskiego i pielgrzymstwa polskiego* [Books of the Polish Nation and the Polish Pilgrimage, 1832]. But let us take into consideration the 1852 edition of *Slávy dcera* [Sláva's

---

1 He arrived in Prague in mid July 1829, accompanied by his friend Kajetan Morozewicz. According to Georges Skvor, while there, he formed the intention of composing a heroic poem on the topic of the Hussite military leader Jan Žižka, a historical character presumably all the more attractive to Mickiewicz, as he fought alongside the Poles in the decisive battle at Grunwald in 1410, when the German Knights of the Cross were finally defeated by the Poles and their allies, under the leadership of King Władysław Jagiełło. See Georges Skvor, 'Le romantisme polonaise et tchèque au XIXe siècle' [Polish and Czech Romanticism in the Nineteenth Century], *Études Slaves et Est-Européennes / Slavic and East-European Studies*, Automne/Autumn 1956, Vol. 1, No. 3, p. 170.

2 For an English translation of this and other works by Štúr, see Ľudovit Štúr, *Slavdom. A Selection of his Writings in Prose and Verse* (London: Glagoslav, 2021).

Daughter], the masterpiece of another great Slovak (or rather, Czechoslovak) poet, Jan Kollár. A gigantic sonnet-cycle conceived along the lines of Dante's *Divina commedia*, the books of which are named for rivers, in this edition, the range is expanded beyond the Slavic streams Laba, Danube and Vltava to encompass the waterways of the great beyond: Lethe (Heaven) and Acheron (Hell). It is no surprise here that, in Kollár's work, Mickiewicz is encountered in the latter, as 'z Paříže ten nevzájemník polský' [that unreciprocating Pole from Paris] is doomed forever to the outer darknesses on account of his inadequate (to put it lightly) Pan-Slavicism.[3]

Of course, Mickiewicz is present here, in Banská Štiavnica, in the best possible way: he is still read. Just the other day, in the used book store on the Námestie Svätej Trojice I found by chance the Czech translation of *Balady a romance*[4] — but no *Slávy dcera*. No Kollár in this Slovak city (I checked two bookstores that same day), but Mickiewicz in pride of place in the poetry section? You can almost hear the unreciprocating Pole from Paris chuckling in Slavic Hell.

One poet you won't have any problem locating in Banská Štiavnica is, of course, Andrej Sládkovič, who spent some ten years of his youth here; it is where he met Mária Geržová, his muse, the inspiration for *Marina* (1844–1846), which, at 2900 lines of verse, is credited as being the longest love-poem ever written.[5] So proud is Banská Štiavnica of this poem, that a museum of sorts devoted to it — the Banka Lásky, or Love Bank — has been established in Mária's old house, just a few metres away from the used book store, on the Radničné námestie. Among the things you can do here is rent a 'deposit box' in the 'love safe,' in which you and your loved one can place an item representing your devotion. For €100 you can take out an 'eternal' lease on a deposit box in the 'love safe,' supposedly *aby Vaša láska trvala večne* [so that your love should last forever]. If you're not quite sure

---

[3] See Jan Kollár, *Slávy dcera. Báseň lyricko-epická v pěti zpěvích* [Sláva's Daughter. A Lyrical-Epic Poem in Five Cantos] (Praha: Nákladem knihkupectví I.L. Kobera, 1868), Sonnet V: 6-9. This sonnet is not included in every edition of the poem.

[4] Adam Mickiewicz, *Balady a romance*, tr. Josef Matouš, František Halas, Vladimír Holan (Praha: Vyšehrad, 1953).

[5] See Pavol Vongrej, *Diamant v hrude. Sládkovičova Marina* [A Diamond in the Rough. Sládkovič's *Marina*] (Martin: Matica slovenská, 1970), p. 99.

of your stamina, patience, or what have you, €50 will buy you a year's rent…
without any such eternal guarantee.⁶

We are are six degrees of separation (or so) from anyone or anything, just about anywhere we are. And so I think it serendipitous that I finished the present translation of *Ballads and Romances*, and am writing the present essay, in Andrej and María's city. For if *Marina* is indeed the longest love poem ever written, *Ballads and Romances*, as a collection almost obsessively dedicated to Mickiewicz's first great love, Maryla Wereszczakówna, might, taken as a whole, be awarded the title of the longest whine ever written. Of the fourteen (1822) or eighteen (1852) poems included herein, a full eleven (1822) or fifteen (1852) deal directly with love (usually unreciprocated, betrayed love, love that leaves at least one broken heart in its wake) — more often than not directly referencing 'Maryla.' That gives us at least 1701, if not 2006, lines of despair, tears, and acidic vituperation. While we can't say 'I see your 2900, and raise you 1701,' it still has to be a record of some sort. One wonders what sort of lease Mickiewicz would have taken out in the Love Bank. And as much as María must have been delighted with the attention she got, it's probably no mystery what Maryla felt…

THE FIRST SALVO OF ROMANTICISM

Ballady i romanse first saw the light of day in Wilno (modern Vilnius, at the time a predominantly Polish city) in 1822. That year, the two-hundredth anniversary of which we are about to celebrate next year (2022 has been designated the 'Year of Romanticism' in Poland) is traditionally considered the starting date for the Romantic Movement in Poland, and *Ballads and Romances*, or *Poetry, Volume I*, as it is sometimes known, has the same sort of significance for Polish Literature that Wordsworth and Coleridge's *Lyrical Ballads* (1798) enjoy in England, or Hugo's *Hernani* (1830) is accorded

---

6   https://bankalasky.sk/objednat-schranku/? [accessed: 24 November 2021]. It's a little too sweet for my tastes, but on reflection, it's a great idea. If only there were such a 'love safe' in my Kraków, perhaps this would relieve some of the weight on the poor Father Bernatek's footbridge, so burdened by 'love locks' (how many of them signifying 'eternal' loves?) that one or two more and it's sure to crumble into the Vistula. What a silly tradition *that* is. And to think of how many keys are now rusting away in the river bottom, poisoning the water, chucked there by the vegan-tribes of fair-trade yerba drinkers wearing non-leather huarache sandals soled with recycled tyre treads!

in French theatre. Although fisticuffs in the 'battle of the Classicists and Romantics,' such as erupted during the première of the French play do not seem to have been too common in Poland, Mickiewicz's first fruits elicited strong reactions on both sides of the issue. As Leonard Chodźko writes in his introduction to the first Paris edition of the poems (1828):

> For several years, Mickiewicz's elemental first poetic attempts have won for him the universal respect of his countrymen and foreigners. It is true that the ardent sectarians of Germanism, starting from the position that a Romantic can do no wrong, for quite some time have indulged the readers of Polish periodicals in exaggerated flights of praise even of the errors of so beautiful a poet, just as the supposed partisans of the classical school, assuming that there can be nothing deserving of praise in Romanticism, have often condemned passages that are actually quite praiseworthy. [...] And yet despite the opposing opinions, the first fruits of Mickiewicz's pen have not ceased to belong among the works most read by the public. Blind jealousy has not been able to tarnish that, which in them is worthy of praise; and that which is blameworthy has not taken on any artificial brilliance due to the unjustified paeans of their equally blind defenders. [...] Sometimes, we find it proper to agree with the Romantics that the greater portion of Mickiewicz's work is deserving of the greatest praise; and yet at times we must also submit to the opinion of the Classicists, taking the poet to task for those parts where, really, in our opinion, they are somewhat blameworthy.[7]

Mickiewicz himself knew what sort of reaction he might expect. Certainly with himself in mind, in his essay 'O poezji romantycznej' [On Romantic Poetry], published in the same year as *Ballads and Romances*, he speaks of a writer who 'foresees, taught by the experiences of others, that his work will meet with condemnation from the very start; perhaps because he chose these, and not those, patterns to follow, and associated himself with this, and not that school.'[8] Even more interesting is his defence of the Romantic

---

7   Leonard Chodźko, 'Przedmowa wydawcy' [Publisher's Introduction], in Adam Mickiewicz, *Poezye, Tom pierwszy* [Poetry. Volume I] (Paris: Barbezat i Delarue, 1828), pp. i, ii, iii.
8   Adam Mickiewicz, 'O poezji romantycznej' [On Romantic Poetry], in Adam

penchant for folk song and folk poetry, upon which his collection is based. It is time to turn away from the *mimesis* of the ancients insisted upon by the Classicists, because 'classicism' — the slavish homage paid to dead texts, divorced from living reality — is not poetry at all. In the ancient world itself, classicism gets underway along with national decadence, when art becomes divorced from the people. It begins with the fall of Greece:

> And then, with the change of circumstances, when the emotions, character, and energy of the nation began to weaken — now by the passage of time, now under the influence of foreigners, now because of public catastrophes, the loss of significance and national freedom — then poetic talent itself ceased to be great, and poetry lost its old character and elevated destiny. The poets parted ways with the people, who no longer had any political significance, and were held in contempt. They took themselves off to the courts of tyrants, there to practise flattery, or weakly, tastelessly, more learnedly than poetically, to imitate the old classical patterns — as can be seen from the examples offered us by the Ptolemaic age. In this way poetry, which once had been a national necessity, was transformed into a game for the erudite, or the lazy.⁹

Today, you will be hard pressed to find anyone willing to express himself in the careful, measured terms employed by Chodźko, to say nothing of taking the poet to task for the 'blameworthy' portions salted through *Ballads and Romances*. Not only has Romanticism won out over the Classical traditions, but poetically speaking, now that time has removed the prism of jealousy through which his contemporaries (as Chodźko suggests) may have examined these works, we can see clearly that — at least as far as the Polish originals are concerned — there is not a weak poem to be found among the fourteen original verses of the 1822 edition, and one of the additional four added in 1852 — 'The Escape' [Ucieczka] is frankly sublime.

Before we go any further, it might be good to make an introductory generic statement in reference to the title of the collection. What is the difference between a ballad and a romance? For there are few, if any, ballads

---

Mickiewicz, *Pisma* [Writings] (Paris–Leipzig: E. Jung Treuttel-Franz Wagner, 1861), Vol. VI, p. 59.
9   Mickiewicz, 'O poezji romantycznej,' pp. 65-66.

in Mickiewicz's collection that fit the common English description of the genre, as a lyric with stanza and refrains. Considering Mickiewicz's book, the two genres seem distinguishable only by their subtitles. However, in his essay 'On Romantic Poetry,' the poet differentiates them thus:

> First among the Italians, it seems, the term *ballad* was used (*canzone a ballo*), which term was applied without differentiation to all sorts of songs of a light, happy nature, which the name itself, deriving from *ballare* (to dance) signifies. Among the Spanish, where folk poetry blossomed healthily, it was known under the name of *Romances*. The French, indeed, differentiated the ballad from other literary genres, not because of essence or character, but rather according to the construction of strophe and verse line. [...] Another character entirely, a clear and enduring one, is possessed by the British ballad. This is a little story woven together from the accidents of common life, or chivalric histories, usually enlivened by the strangeness of the romantic world, sung in a melancholic tone, in a serious style, simple and natural in its expressions. [...] The romance (*romanza*) is similar to the ballad. Widespread especially in Spain and France, it is all the more different from the ballad in that it is dedicated to tenderness; uncanny imagination has a lesser influence upon it, and generally, speaking of form, it tends to the dramatic. Its style, on the other hand, ought to appeal through the greatest simplicity and naiveté.[10]

Mickiewicz does not include the Polish or Slavic traditions here — perhaps because he was fully aware of the fact that it was beginning with him, now.[11] Somewhat problematic to our understanding of these generic issues may be his reference to an enlivening 'by the strangeness of the romantic world.'

---

10   Mickiewicz, 'O poezji romantycznej,' pp. 88-90.

11   Very insightfully, Kazimierz Cysewski suggests that the first poem in the collection, 'Pierwiosnek' [The Primrose], as a poem about the first blooms of spring, is a metaphor of the collection as a whole being the first bloom of the Romantic spring to come in Poland. See Kazimierz Cysewski, '*Ballady i romanse* — przewodnik epistemologiczny' [*Ballads and Romances* — an Epistemological Guide], *Pamiętnik Literacki: czasopismo kwartalne poświęcone historii i krytyce literatury polskiej*, 74/3 (1983), p. 66.

What does he mean when he says 'romantic?' The best answer to this may be given in the poems themselves, especially the poem so titled.

When one speaks of the programmatic nature of *Ballads and Romances*, it is usually the second poem, 'Romanticism' [Romantyczność] which initiates, and sometimes concludes, the discussion. One would be hard put to find a more fitting metaphor of the cognitive impasse between the cold reason of the Enlightenment and the more open attitudes of Romanticism, than that of Karusia, the young girl complaining to the ghost of her dead lover:

> [Here] I'm surrounded on all hands
> By evil folk, who mock and jeer —
> I speak, and no one understands.
> No one can see what I see, clear!

It is commonplace to state that, whereas the Enlightenment saw the reason as the only avenue to understanding the world around us, the Romantics returned to a more holistic, and perhaps more human and psychologically true, conception of cognition, according to which the reason (never completely rejected, after all), is supplemented by intuition and revelation. The spiritual world is given a place at the table once again, after its brief banishment during 'the long eighteenth century;' a spiritual world that, in Romanticism, ranges from the Gothic interest in ghost stories through the passion for the Gothic Age of Faith, which resulted in many a conversion to that most 'irrational' form of Christianity, Roman Catholicism, during this time.

In 'Romanticism,' the Age of Reason pokes its unsightly nose into the story in the person of the 'wiseman,' the rationalist scholar with his 'microscope,' who deems Karusia insane and scolds the people of the village for 'blaspheming against reason.' While — as Goethe does with *Erlkönig* — Mickiewicz deftly describes the scene so that we, the readers, are given no concrete evidence either way (is the ghost of Jasieńko there indeed, or is poor Karusia merely hallucinating?), because of the narrator's final assessment of the matter, and, perhaps, our own position as the heirs of Romanticism, we tend to side with the girl, rather than the cold, and somewhat bitter, professor.[12] For even her youth (in contrast to the advanced age of the

---

12 The 'wiseman' in question was Jan Śniadecki, a professor of the University of Wilno, and an ardent opponent of Romanticism and Shakespeare (hence the poem's motto from *Hamlet*). See Jacek Brzozowski, 'Głosy do "Romantyczności"'

professor) or her madness (even if that were the case) would not sway the Romantic, or us, to his side. The Romantics, and, I assert, we their descendants, are more than willing to accept the Psalmist's statement: 'Out of the mouth of infants and of sucklings thou hast perfected praise.'[13] For the Romantics, children and the mad can also be oracles, conduits of wisdom.

The pious villagers — was it they who earlier 'mocked and jeered' the young girl? — are willing to entertain the possibility that her prematurely deceased intended has come back to visit her, and fall to their knees in prayer. The narrator does as well, and in his direct address to the rationalist, he expresses himself in lines that quickly became one of the battlecries of Romanticism in Poland:

> 'The child feels,' I answer humbly. 'Truly,
> Those simple people have great faith and hope.
> Feeling and faith speak more profoundly to me
> Than wise-man's eye and ground-glass microscope.
>
> 'You know dead truths, as you dissect and sunder
> Planets to atoms, stars to sparks; your art
> Grasps no live truth. You'll never glimpse a wonder
> Unless you feel, and gaze into the heart!'

In short, we have here the Romantic conviction of the existence of truths outside the range of empirical research. How much more nuanced an attitude this is, than that of Khrushchev and his cosmonauts, who ham-handedly declared that they 'had not noticed God' during their orbits!

Still and all, although from our perspective there is nothing surprising, threatening, or even novel about the Romantic approach to things, all men

---

[Glosses to 'Romanticism'], *Prace Polonistyczne*, seria XLIX (1994): 7-48, p. 18. Mickiewicz's stripe of Romanticism has a healthy distaste for over-intellectualism that excludes spiritual wonder from all equations. The word *mędrzec* [wiseman, though with overtones of 'wiseacre'] is one of the most bitter epithets in his vocabulary. In his greatest work, the monumental drama *Dziady* [Forefathers' Eve], his hero Konrad even rails against God Himself for cold intellectualism, and threatens to do battle with Him at 'heart's-point.' For an English translation, see: Adam Mickiewicz, *Forefathers' Eve* (London: Glagoslav, 2016), Part III, scene ii (the 'Great Improvisation').

13   Psalm 8:2.

are creatures of their upbringing, and feel most comfortable in their familiar reality. Thus, Mickiewicz's full frontal assault on exclusive rationality in the name of spirit, as we find in the ballad 'This I Like' [To Lubię], must have been a shock to more than one system in the Poland of 1822:

> As soon as midnight draws its gloomy pall
>   Above, the church doors open with a crash;
> In empty belfry bells begin to toll
>   And something thumps and hisses through that patch
>
> Where sometimes a pale light is seen to glow.
>   Bolt after thunderbolt flashes and booms;
> Grave-lids are pressed up, slid off from below,
>   And ghosts are seen to spill out of the tombs.
>
> A headless corpse now down the pathway strolls;
>   And there a severed head speedily hies,
> Champing its jaws as through the dust it rolls
>   With flaming sockets where had once been eyes.

No wonder some of the rationalist wags, who could formulate sharp *pointes* like few others, reacted to this sort of thing with the punning *Ciemno wszędzie, głucho wszędzie / Głupstwo było, głupstwo będzie*.[14]

Now we began talking about love, and we will continue to do so. As far as 'Romanticism' itself is concerned, this is, as far as the plot goes, a poem about the love of one human being for another: Karusia's love for Jasieńko, and, ultimately, vice versa. But more importantly — and this is why Mickiewicz's ballads and romances are more than (to speak metaphorically) pop songs — it is about a greater love, that which binds the whole human race together, all of its generations, the past as well as the present. Here we need to talk about

---

14 'Everywhere dark, everywhere silent / Idiocy always was, idiocy always will be.' The lines, which rhyme in Polish, are a travesty of a famous refrain from Mickiewicz's *Forefathers' Eve*, where pious folk, gathered for a semi-Christian evocation of the souls of the dead, chant *Ciemno wszędzie, głucho wszędzie / Co to będzie? Co to będzie?* [Everywhere dark, everywhere silent / What will happen? What will happen?] See Adam Mickiewicz, *Forefathers' Eve*, Part II.

MICKIEWICZ AND THE DANTEAN TRADITION.

One of the facts in the poem that we can point to as evidence that Karusia isn't mad, after all, is her equivocal reaction to the appearance of her departed lover's ghost. Like any person in his right mind, she is unsure, and frightened:

> '[...] ...Now that you're gone,
> You're dead and buried, life goes on,
> They say — You're dead, Jasieńko! And I'm scared!
> But if it's you, I'm frightened? Why?
> It's you! That same cheek, that same eye —
> That same white shirt you wear!
>
> 'And you — white as a sheet as well,
> And cold... How cold the hands I grip!
> Come, I'll press you to my breast a spell,
> And hold you tight — lip to lip!

She's attended the funeral of the young man she was supposed to wed at that same altar; she's seen him dead. Thus, when he suddenly appears before her, her first reaction, as we say, is fright. 'You're dead, Jasieńko! And I'm scared!' But notice what she says immediately thereafter: 'But if it's you, I'm frightened? Why?' And then, after she gets a better look at him, and recognises his identity for sure, she bursts into joy and concern. What we need to concentrate on here is the manner in which Mickiewicz handles the sudden appearance — not of a ghost, a dead person — but the ghost of a loved one, the return of a lover, a friend, from beyond the grave. Should one of our departed family members or friends suddenly appear at our threshold, literally out of the blue, why on earth should we assume that this person, who loved us during his or her earthly life, was now coming with malicious or hateful intent? That makes no sense at all. Karusia has every right to be startled, and even a little scared, at the start — such is only human. Appearances like this don't happen all the time. And yet, when she recognises, not only the reality of the unusual phenomenon facing her, but the identity of the ghost, she is calm, and full of concern for her lover's cold limbs — and reacts just as she would had he arrived at her cottage door alive, in the winter time, poorly dressed.

This is much more than the (trite but true) saying that 'love lasts beyond the grave.' It is at the heart of the Catholic faith from which Mickiewicz, Dante before him, and Eliot after him, spring:[15] the conviction that death is not only not the end of life, but that, in the Communion of the Saints (to which all traditional Christians confess during the recitation of the Nicene Creed), we, the Church Militant — the living — have a responsibility towards the Church Suffering — the souls in Purgatory. We must care for them and pray for them, so as to shorten their time spent in that place of suffering and joy, and spring them into the full joy of Heaven. To complete the cycle, let us remind ourselves that when they arrive there, among the saints in glory — the Church Triumphant — they will pray for us here below. And so, just as the Communion of the Saints, which is the motor behind both Dante's *Divine Comedy* and Mickiewicz's masterpiece, *Forefathers' Eve* is really a wheel of love, always in motion, so Mickiewicz's take on love, here in *Ballads and Romances* as well, is that of a broader love than mere 'boy meets girl.'

Parts II and IV of *Forefathers' Eve*, which were to be published shortly after *Ballads and Romances*, only one year later, as a matter of fact, in 1823, begin with the semi-pagan, semi-Christian folk ritual of evoking the spirits of the recently dead — with the aim of learning exactly what it is they need in order to enter the full happiness of Heaven, and finish with the main character's — Gustaw himself is a revenant spirit — appeal to us not to forget the souls suffering in Purgatory. And so, the villagers' immediate falling to their knees in prayer for the spirit they cannot see is much more than an expression of sympathy for the poor girl — it is a pious, good work, and a belated one at that, if they had earlier mocked her; reparations for their ignorance, their heartlessness, which is no less wrong than that of the 'wiseman.' Likewise, Karusia's desire to 'warm' the limbs of her frigid betrothed is more than a sweet, innocent gesture, it is a visible sign of her orientation to the Communion of the Saints — a sacrament.

The great characteristic of all of Mickiewicz's 'otherworldly' Romanticism is the manner in which he plays with us — leading us into expecting

---

15   For a discussion of the Catholic underpinnings of Mickiewicz's signature work, *Forefathers' Eve*, see Katarzyna Lukas' discussion of Part IV in her 'Der romantische Protagonist als Träger des katholischen Weltbildes. Über den IV. Teil des dramatischen Fragments Dziady von Adam Mickiewicz in deutschsprachigen Übersetzungen,' *Studia Germanica Posnaniensia*, XXX (2006), pp. 5-33. What she says there has a wider application to his entire oeuvre.

a run-of-the-mill Gothic narrative of devils and evil spirits just waiting to pounce upon the unwary 'innocent' victim, only to uncover a different, benign, even holy aspect of the world of wonders — hidden from our sight, but at our elbow all the time.

Consider these introductory stanzas from 'Świteź' — that lake now within the borders of Belarus, which forms the backdrop to so many of these poetic narratives:

> For what dark revels there the devils hold!
>   What ghosts and spectres shriek throughout the night!
> To hear the old folks' tales, my blood runs cold,
>   And till the blessed dawn I quake in fright.
>
> Sometimes the lake's aflame; thick billows rise
>   Of smoke — it seems as if a city swarms
> Within: and quarrels, shouts, and women's cries,
>   Bells frenzied peal, amidst the clash of arms.
>
> Then — sudden calm; the firestorm disappears
>   And nothing but fir-sighing fills the air.
> Deep, muffled voices is all that one hears;
>   That, and a girl — sobbing a mournful prayer.

The fame of the place, whether misunderstood or embellished for the good of the story, turns out to be far from the truth. Whatever sort of phenomena are beheld there in the depths of night, the 'dark revels of the devils' have nothing to do with them. The 'girl, sobbing a mournful prayer' will appear shortly to the audacious young squire who determines to get to the bottom (literally) of the myth, and reveal a tragic tale that tends — despite it all — to the mercy and grace of God. Indeed, there exists more than that, which is found in our philosophy — especially given our penchant to make mistakes.

Mickiewicz scholar Michał Kuziak sees a sensitivity to the sublime as a characteristic of Mickiewicz's poetic makeup. He is spot-on when he suggests that the rapture that the poet senses when faced with overwhelming natural phenomena (in this particular case, he is discussing one of the poet's *Crimean Sonnets*, on the narrow mountain pass in Chufut-Kale) is not mere exaltation at the beauties of God's creation, but an intimation of the spiritual glory, which far surpasses the natural, and therefore is difficult for us to comprehend while in the flesh:

> Sublimity, being a sign of mystery, of limitlessness, discloses also the limitations of the human person, the existence of a dimension that goes beyond the cognitive possibilities of reason (constituting on the other hand the object of experience), and, as such, ineffable, impossible to express in speech.[16]

Mickiewicz is not a writer of horror stories. To return to the ballad at hand, we would state that the common denominator to his otherworldly tales (if they may be called such, given that they take place here and now, in our reality) is that what appears to be diabolical and dreadful is often something benign, even benevolent. The Świtezianka turns out to be a victim — with a message.

But more of that later. The same situation is found in 'This I Like,' the poem with which we began our study of the uncanny in *Ballads and Romances*. When the area in which the encounter between narrator and 'Maryla's' ghost will take place is described, the narrator wonders, is this 'the haunt of demon, or of cursèd soul?' Actually, neither, because the soul in question is suffering, not diabolical, and in Purgatory, not Hell, and thus must be prayed for, to be released from her torment. When the narrator breathes out — quite unconsciously, almost as an expletive — 'This I like!' the dead woman's penance has run its course, she becomes visible, and, in response to the startled narrator's ejaculation 'Let Christ's Name be forever praised!' responds 'Forever and ever.' Just as in 'Świteź' no evil sprite would pray, so here: no demon or damned spirit would praise Christ. She is no hound of hell, but 'a repentant soul, / Who soon shall bask in everlasting bliss.' The reality, again, is proven diametrically different from what people assume.

It is curious — and in a literary sense extraordinarily effective — that the narrator releases her only by accident. Had he not been in the habit of tossing off the ironic phrase 'This I like!' when faced by an irritating setback, and in her hearing, her torments would not have ended, her haunting of the lonely road near the bridge never brought to a happy conclusion.

---

16 Michał Kuziak, *Inny Mickiewicz* [Another Mickiewicz] (Gdańsk: Słowo/Obraz terytoria, 2013), p. 57.

Her situation, therefore, was tragic. If she's haunting the people, according to her own account, this is only because such is part of her penance: to beg for prayers in a manner that will bring about the opposite result. As the narrator tells us, setting the stage for the encounter:

> Each traveller would fain avoid this road;
>   None travel here but leaves behind a curse
> For broken wagon-tongues, overturned load,
>   Sprained oxen-legs and spooked or hobbled horse.

Their reactions through the years (according to Maryla's own account, she has been dead for a century) are quite understandable. But — and this is the point — they have some share in guilt as well. Let us return for a moment to the citation above from stanza three, in which the narrator wonders is this the 'haunt of demons or of curséd soul?' He responds in the very next line: 'No one remembers,' and there's the rub! A young woman has died, and no one remembers her. At her individual judgment (which waits upon us all at the moment of our death), she was not damned to hell, rather, she was assigned to Purgatory, a place of blessedness (for all who are in Purgatory now will one day be in Heaven; there is no 'down' escalator from there!) and suffering too — but suffering in a way that can be relieved by the living, shortening the soul's sojourn in the realm of purgation, through their prayers. While it may not be surprising that she is no longer remembered by the present generation, ten full decades after her demise, what does this say about the parents she mentions in her account, and all the other people who knew her during her lifetime? Why did they 'forget' her so soon, and their duty towards her? This is the charge that Mickiewicz places at the feet of her family and the people of the area. Again, we are enjoined to remember the dead and pray for them — if they had prayed for the repose of her soul, they would never have been haunted in the first place.

This theme of criminal forgetfulness, of how quick we are to forget the sorrows and needs of others, is continued in 'The Minstrel' [Dudarz]. There, when the wandering old singer, a stranger to the parts in which his story plays out, intones a song of heartbreak,

> A murmur rumbles then, a rumour darts
>   Among the crowd — a pallor falls.

> That song was heard around these parts
> Before — but when? And who? No one recalls.

Once more, a foggy memory is jogged — that of an unfortunate boy who, through unreciprocated love, left their village, never to be seen again, to die far away in foreign parts. When they had the chance to help him, they didn't. Soon, he was forgotten, even by his friends and relatives. Even if they had remained unable to give him what he wanted — his 'Maryla,' for who could do that, if Maryla herself didn't wish it — still they might have done something for him, anything, so that he wouldn't have withered away on a distant, barren strand, his heartache eating at him like a cancer, to be neglected in life and in death. As the singer presents his ballad, it is as if a ghost had uprisen before the villagers now, accusing them of heartless unconcern when he, suffering, was among them.

In Mickiewicz's works, *Ballads and Romances* as well as *Forefathers' Eve*, the cycle of love which is the Communion of the Saints is not only shown spinning in the direction of the Church Militant toward the Church Suffering. The villagers of Part II of *Forefathers' Eve* do not only seek to lighten the sufferings of the souls they invoke; they learn from them. Part III begins with a representative of the Church Triumphant — Gustaw/Konrad's guardian angel, at the behest of the character's sainted mother — arriving at the sleeping man's bedside in prison to aid his charge along his progress through this life. Likewise, in the poem under discussion now, 'This I Like,' the young woman, released from her purgative suffering, turns to the narrator with:

> The while the stars yet shine, before the crow
>   Of the first rooster, I will here relate
> My story — which the faithful ought to know
>   So they might take a lesson from my fate.

As with the information culled from the souls Dante encounters on his journeys, as in the 'teachings' imparted to the villagers in *Forefathers' Eve* by the souls they summon in order to aid them, so here, in repayment for his good deed in — even unconsciously — releasing her from Purgatory into Heaven, the new saint will bestow on us, through him, the wisdom of her story, which will aid us, if we listen carefully, to avoid the mistakes she made and progress more surely and painlessly through this life towards a better reward.

This is the most striking thing about Adam Mickiewicz's *Ballads and Romances* in particular, and all his literary works in general. It is also the place where he and Dante meet and shake hands. The *Divine Comedy* of Dante Alighieri is a literary work of its own genre. No one believes that the story Dante tells — that of his journey through the three realms of Hell, Purgatory and Heaven, to return back to earth (and to us, the community from which he departed in that 'dark wood') ever really took place. The *Divine Comedy* is a fiction, but a fiction with a purpose. Through it, Dante conveys to us a great truth, the most important truth of our human existence, that of our inevitable death, and what comes after. How often does he halt the stream of his narrative to turn to us, directly, with words on the order of, 'if only you were able to see with your eyes what I see with mine, you would be moved to a reformation of your life!' In this, the use of fiction in order to convey a truth of cosmic proportions, essential to every man and woman, Dante's *Divine Comedy* is a unique work, generically comparable only to the Gospels.

In a similar way, Adam Mickiewicz's *Ballads and Romances* are not written with mere entertainment in mind, but also to spur us, their readers, to better action. And in this way, Adam Mickiewicz stands out from all other poets of his generation in Europe. And so, curiously enough, despite the revulsion that some of the Classicists felt for his work when it first appeared two hundred years ago, as Leonard Chodźko tells us in his introduction, Mickiewicz is not that far from the *docere dulce* literary ideal of the Age of Reason. He just wishes, teaching sweetly through his poetry, to impart to us a greater knowledge.

Mickiewicz is the creator of the great tradition of Polish Monumental Drama, in which spirits of the dead appear among the living and interact with them. This theatre is based upon the Christian conviction of the continuation of life after death, which is expressed in the verses that make up *Ballads and Romances* as well. His view of reality is like two intersecting circles, one representing temporal reality and the other eternity, and, as long as time exists, as long as the world exists, we live out our lives on the shaded area of that Venn diagram, with spirits all around us. And the message that he has for us does not concern any 'chain of being' such as we find in the writings of Alexander Pope, but rather the spiritual reality of the afterlife to which all of us, living in that shaded area of action and responsibility, deed and reward, are tending.

JUSTICE HERE AND NOW

Just as the warnings and lessons provided by these emissaries of eternity are intended to be made use of by us here on this earth, in this present time, so a frequent theme of *Ballads and Romances* is the settling of scores here and now. Justice — especially for sins against love, broadly conceived — is served hot; it does not arrive with leaden feet; the mills of Mickiewicz's folk justice spin quickly indeed. The young woodsman in the ballad 'The Świtezianka' learns this quickly, and too late. Long the lover of a water nymph, whom he has sworn always to love, he fails horribly when his troth is put to the test:

> Then a sudden breeze blows, and disperses the mist;
> What had been hid therein now's uncovered:
> And he sees... that the maiden he'd striven to kiss
> Is... the girl... is... his abandoned lover!
>
> 'So then, this is how you vows and promises keep?
> Remember my words? Now your role
> In this life is to moan and incessantly weep,
> And then — woe to your foul, faithless soul!'

It is worth noting here that, as we mentioned above, here too we see Mickiewicz taking a common theme of folklore and modifying it. The Świtezianka is no evil Rusalka, the familiar siren of Slavic mythology, who uses her charms to (sadistically) tempt the unwary yokel to a watery grave for no good reason except her desire to do evil, but a sentient being who can be loved, and is no less deserving of good faith and devotion as any human wife. Reading through Mickiewicz's poem, we do not take the side of the woodsman, our own kind, but rather that of the water nymph. Our sympathies lie with the wronged party (she was betrayed by the man who swore to love her, but would abandon her for erotic play with someone he took to be a willing, different partner), and we come away with the feeling that justice was served — he got just what was coming to him.

For the spiritual world — God, justice, however you choose to name it — is not cruel and sadistic; it makes the sinner pay, evening the score after the initial crime. Folk justice, as depicted in Mickiewicz's *Ballads and Romances* is no less fitting than the *contrapassi* we come across tormenting the sinners in Dante's *Inferno*. To give just two examples from the Italian masterpiece, thieves are punished by being condemned to seek to escape reptiliform spirits. Once these capture one of the anthropoid souls of those condemned for thievery, a grotesque metamorphosis takes place: the two bodies meld until that which had been a reptile, takes on the human form of its prey, and that which had been of human appearance, becomes a reptile — at which the chase begins anew, the hunter having become the hunted, on and on. The poetic justice is obvious. It is a repetition of the money-lust and fear that characterised the thief during life: first the chase after and appropriation of someone else's goods, and then the feverish, paranoid escape with the loot, which the thief is always in fear of having taken away from him again. Similarly, the suicides. For whatever reason, Dante holds this group of sinners in the greatest disdain. They are the only damned whom he deprives of the dignity of human form. Upon death, condemned for their extreme contempt of the body (the image and likeness of God), they are chucked over the shoulder of the diabolical judge to whom they present themselves and wherever they land, they take root as trees. Even at the resurrection of the flesh, when (to augment the bliss of Heaven or the sufferings of Hell), our mortal bodies will be returned to us, Dante's suicides will also receive theirs. But not to be clothed in them again — they will remain trees for all eternity, and the bodies that are returned to them will be suspended from their branches by the neck.

In just this way, consider the justice meted out to poor Krysia in 'The Little Fish' [Rybka]. Wronged by the lord of the manor, who had his way with her, got her pregnant, and then abandoned her to marry a 'princess,' she rushes off to a streamlet that feeds Lake Świteź and, halting at the brink, calls out:

> 'O my sisters, Świteź maidens, dear,
>   Who in the lake waters swirl,
> Swim close now, my darlings! And give ear
>   To the plaint of a scorned girl!
>
> [...]
>
> 'Sisters, I come — what now restrains me?
>   But... oh my child! Oh, my child!'

> She says no more, no — but how she weeps!
>   Then she closes her eyes tight,
> Steps close to the brink, and then she leaps!
>   The stream bears her out of sight.

Do we feel sorry for Krysia? Yes. Is she a victim, wronged by a cad? Absolutely. Was she right in deciding to commit suicide? No! What should have restrained her from taking the fatal plunge? She answers her question in the very next line: her child. Dante teaches us that suicide is a sin thrice over: it is a sin against oneself (obviously), a sin against God (like trampling on a crucifix, for example, it is a vulgar spurning of the image and likeness of God) and — is this why Dante is so unforgiving towards suicides? Did he have a personal experience with this? — it is a sin against one's brethren. For even if the self-murder 'ends the sufferings' of the suicide him- or herself, it only *initiates* the suffering of all those who loved the suicide, condemning them to a life of mourning and sadness at a death which is not only untimely, but naggingly inappropriate, unnecessary, avoidable. And if that is true for the self-murder of anyone we love, how much more must it be true for mothers who abandon their children in this manner?

And so, she too will be punished — the balance must be restored — and despite our sympathy for her, we acknowledge the punishment as just. It must be pointed out here that Krysia's situation is not the same as that of the Świtezianka just discussed. Although she addresses the water nymphs as her 'sisters,' she is a human being of flesh and blood, something proven, at the very least, in the third stanza cited above. If she were a creature of the waters, and an ondine herself, returning to her native, watery element, why would she 'close her eyes tight' in fear as she does so? No, only a real girl, driven to suicide in her despair, would close her eyes tight in fear of the unnatural act she was about to commit.

This is an important point, for it clearly foregrounds both the inexorable nature of eternal justice and that frail human incomprehension of things that constitutes another theme of the *Ballads and Romances*. For Krysia, in her naiveté, does not believe that ending her life in the river will lead to oblivion, an end to her woes in non-existence. The thought would never cross her mind. There were very few atheists or nihilists among the folk of Mickiewicz's day. No, she believes in something even more incomprehensible. By throwing herself into the current, she thinks that she will not merely be crossing over from our temporal world into eternity, but that she will be exchanging the quotidian world of existence on land, among bipedal betrayers like her seducer, for a purer existence in the parallel world under the surface of Lake Świteź. She believes, without any basis in reality to believe such a thing, that she will cease being a woman of flesh and blood to become a water nymph herself — a sister among sisters. Not only is this impossible in a physical sense (rationalistically speaking), it is impossible in a spiritual sense. Suicide, like the abandonment of one's child, is a sin. Justice demands punishment for such acts, not a *reward*, such as a transformation into a Świtezianka would be.

And so, of course, her existence does continue after death, but, in a logical *contrapasso*, that would be in a state that is less than envious. When the peasant lad who takes pity on her abandoned child arrives at the riverside in despair, calling for her, wondering aloud who will suckle the infant now that her mother has disappeared (again — she is *sinning selfishly*[17] in thinking of her own present woe, seeing in it a greater wrong to be redressed than the future hardship to which she is condemning her infant), she replies:

> 'I'm here — beneath the rushing river,'
> [...]
> 'The icy current makes me shiver,
>   The gravel pummels my eyes.
>
> 'Over the rough-pebbled river-bed
>   The currents batter me blue;
> On coral and fly-larva I'm fed,
>   My drink is the frigid dew.'

So much for a promotion up a grade to the spiritual condition of a water nymph! And yet, to justice mercy is coupled. Like that of Maryla from 'This I Like,' the suffering of Krysia in 'The Little Fish' is purgatorial; the debt can be paid off, and will be. She is not in Hell, but Purgatory. For much excuses Krysia's behaviour, however blameworthy it may be; she was driven

---

17   Although the tone of his book is often sardonic, Jan Walc hits the nail right on the head when, in his discussion of the Purgatorial souls summoned to Dziady in Part II of *Forefathers' Eve*, he notes: 'And yet there is something that binds all of the sinners, whose souls have arrived at the Forefathers' Eve ceremony, together — their introspection, their living for themselves alone, without a care for others.' Jan Walc, *Architekt Arki* [The Architect of the Ark] (Chotomów: Verba, 1991), p. 36.

to this drastic action by being sinned against herself. For her story does not end here, as a monitory tale warning us not to presume as she did. Krysia is allowed to suckle to her child, cosseting him when he arrives at the riverside with the peasant boy, his new guardian. Although the transformation of the fish into mermaid (and vice versa) is described in rather grotesque terms by Mickiewicz (as one final, apt, reminder that Krysia's transformation is a punishment, not an elevation), the fact that she is allowed to resume a half-woman, mermaid existence, and nourish the child she abandoned (spending some time with him, which must soothe her mother's heart), indicates that she is not a damned creature, but a 'repentant soul.'

The real punishment is reserved for the perfidious man and his bride. One day, arriving late to the banks of the stream, the peasant lad finds Krysia's seducer and his bride strolling there. The boy hides, and after a long while during which they were not returning, he finally makes his way out of the brambles to find that the stream has disappeared, and in its place:

> Bits of clothing were strewn alongside
>   Where the shore had once been, there;
> Yet neither groom, nor his princess bride
>   Were to be seen anywhere!
>
> And then — his heart thumped — and he stood stock-
>   Still — there, where once rushed the stream,
> Loomed, in the moonlight, a lump of rock —
>   Like two bodies, fused, it seemed.

It also seems that Krysia had her role to play in this meting out of justice. Before her plunge, she warned her seducer and his wife not to 'mock' her, and the peasant lad, at the end of the poem, understands that it was she who effected their Dantean transformation into rock.[18] If this is the case, and it certainly seems to be, given the manner in which the ballad closes, Krysia, herself punished by justice, becomes an executor of a justly-meted

---

[18] Or, one might also say Ovidian transformation. As in the case of Lycaon, who was not so much transformed into a wolf, as his metamorphosis was actually a revealing of the bloodthirsty inner nature he possessed while still in human form, so here: their transformation into cold stone is a mere revealing of the cold, stony hearts that beat in their breasts while still human.

sentence upon other sinners (even worse ones, it seems), and thus she has also become part of the 'righteous' otherworld.

Now, it might be asked, what is the sin of the seducer's *bride*? Why is she punished, and so severely? And how is the seducer's abandonment of Krysia — did he even know she was pregnant and had given birth to his child? — any more unforgivable than her own abandonment of the baby? Without getting into speculation here, theological or literary, we can say that, if suicide is the sin that Dante (not God) seems to hate most, it is obvious that in *Ballads and Romances* pride of place in this regard is held by erotic infidelity. Once again, in 'The Little Fish,' we have a tale of broken vows. And both the seducer and his princess bride (usurping Krysia's place) are guilty of that. How tempting it is to see Mickiewicz wagging his finger here in warning at Maryla!

More of that later. Let us bring this section of our discussion on justice to an end with a reference to the ballad 'Papa's Return' [Powrót Taty]. In this poem, the worried wife of a merchant absent too long from home begs her children to go out to the crossroads and pray before an image of Our Lady for his safe deliverance from harm. It turns out that her fears were justified, as a group of bandits, learning that he would pass this way, richly laden with goods, had determined to ambush him. However, the leader of the band has mercy on the merchant, and spares his life. When the reprieved Papa thanks him:

'[...] Spare your breath!'
 The bandit glares with angry eye.
'Long since you would have tasted death
 If not for... Let me tell you why.

'It's these your children you should thank
 That thus your life I deign to spare.
For, lurking here beneath this bank,
 I heard them raise their humble prayer.

'I knew that you would pass this way,
 A merchant, laden with rich goods,
And so I set a trap today
 To kill and plunder — So I should,

'If not for their incessant prayers.
 At first I laughed in spirit, jeered...
But then, some feelings, unawares
 Crept through my soul. I shrank with fear...

'For I recalled my distant home
 And sensed mercy begin to sway
My heart — I've a wife of my own,
 And son — who's no older than they.

'So, merchant! Be off to your city.
 I, to the woods, stained with my crimes;
Children, I beg you — of your pity,
 Recall me in your prayers sometimes.'

Speaking of the didactic aspect of *Ballads and Romances*, of the messages given to the protagonists who appear in them and then relayed to us, the readers, this is one of the more powerful. For, it appears that there is nothing supernatural about the denouement of this story — nothing overtly miraculous: neither God nor angel intervenes. Rather, the bandit hears the children's prayers and is moved, made better by the actions of people performed in innocence of heart, people completely unaware of an audience. And so, the motto: act well always, for you never know who's watching you, what influence you might have on others.

This is a message, I venture, worth keeping in mind, and in this particular ballad, which has nothing to do with erotic love or any Maryla, the receptor Mickiewicz has in mind is you and me. As we have seen, the application of *Ballads and Romances* is much broader than is often assumed in the traditional critical shorthand that sees in it the first great love cycle in Polish Romanticism — Poland's *Marina*. Of course, it's not hard to see why this is so; even a cursory reading of *Ballads and Romances* reveals to one's eye the poet's fascination — obsession? — with

MARYLA, MARYLA, AND ONLY MARYLA.

To what extent did the historical Maryla — Marianna Ewa Puttkamerowa (née Wereszczakówna, 1799–1863) — the great, tragic love of Adam Mickiewicz's life, his muse, his Beatrice, in short, the mythical Maryla of legend — inspire the immortal poetry he went on to create? Anything that sounds so much like a Harlequin Romance cannot be entirely true, and scholars such as Jan Walc have done their best to 'de-bronzify' the legend.[19] Others, like the scholar Grzegorz Szelwach, delving into Mickiewicz's letters, show the 'bard' to have been, at times, something of a calculating literary businessman, who knew a good, saleable story when he saw one.[20]

It is impossible to know, I reckon, how much the constant references to 'Maryla' and the narrator's 'broken heart' found in *Ballads and Romances* are a record of the poet's actual experience, and how much they are a mere literary construct. That his erotic experience with her was authentic — of whatever sort it was — is proven by a letter written to a friend after his final parting with her:

> I knew that her feelings were not of the same nature as mine, that I had lost her; I know what will become of her and what of me, and I do not think her very unhappy. You are mistaken when you assume that I am saddened by her happiness, and that sadness becomes me [...] I wish her all the happiness in the world, sincerely, well, perhaps not *all* happiness; I wish myself enough so that she would be happy, and for this reason I don't want to find out about everything.[21]

What is most likely — and I think this can be sensed even from the calm manner in which he discusses the affair in this fragment above — *Ballads and Romances* are both autobiographical confession (to a certain extent)

---

19   See his *Architekt Arki*, mentioned above.

20   See Grzegorz Szelwach, *Listy Adama Mickiewicza* [The Letters of Adam Mickiewicz] (New York: PIASA Books, 2006). People have a tendency to look at their artistic heroes, especially poets, as some sort of elevated beings, if not disembodied spirits. The great virtue of Szelwach's book is the presentation of these personal writings of the Bard, which reveal him to be a likeable, normal person. While they show the young Mickiewicz to be a fellow with his feet firmly on the ground, they also reveal, stirringly, some mystical experiences that — why should we disbelieve them? — give credence to the legend of the great Polish Romantic as an authentically inspired, if not to say prophetic, voice.

21   Mickiewicz, Letter to Onufry Pietraszkiewicz dated 13/25 IX 1821. Cited in Szelwach, pp. 72–73.

and literary construct. While the two are not mutually exclusive in the least, we are, after all, dealing with a literary work, and not a diary.

If there is any truth to the 'Wereszczakówna' thesis, there yet remains the question: Are *Ballads and Romances* an obsessive tribute to Maryla? Or is the collection an angry, nearly Catullus-like, diatribe against her for dumping him? Whatever the case may be, a reading shows that the attitude of the overarching narrator (whether we identify him with the poet or not) to the Maryla who appears in the background of the collection (whether she be Count Wawrzyniec Puttkamer's intended or not), is one of bitter reproach. The tone is struck in the very first poem of the collection, 'The Primrose' [Pierwiosnek]. It is the flower speaking to the narrator:

> Am I worthy your sweetheart? Say,
>   What do you think, Marylka, dear?
> When he gave you a primrose spray
>   You paid him back... with his first tears!

The bitterness continues in 'This I Like.' Here, the ghost of the woman redeemed from Purgatory by the narrator's unconscious exclamation introduces herself:

> 'In those days, when my living lungs respired
>   This atmosphere, Maryla was my name;
> My father was the first man of the shire:
>   Wealthy, and honest, of unspotted fame.
>
> 'His greatest longing was to see me married.
>   That I was young and well-endowed, a scurry
> Of lovers hastened — yes, no suitor tarried
>   To vie for my charms — and my dowery.
>
> 'So many men to stroke my vanity!
>   In their vain blandishments I so delighted,
> The lower they bowed, my inanity
>   Swelled the greater, as I scorned them all, and slighted.'

Very similar she is to Maryla Wereszczakówna, that young provincial beauty coming of the lesser, but notable, provincial nobility, both sword and distaff, boasting the 'Kościesza' coat of arms. The fact that Mickiewicz names her 'Maryla,' even though she precedes his lover by a century or more, is significant, and cannot have been lost upon her, or upon the contemporaries who knew them both. But even more significant is the reason for her purgatorial punishment: 'So many men to stroke my vanity! [...] The lower they bowed, my inanity / Swelled the greater, as I scorned them all, and slighted.' Whatever may be the truth behind Walc's statement that Maryla's 'erotic knowledge was not limited to romance narratives,'[22] there is no evidence that Maryla Wereszczakówna-Puttkamerowa was a particularly sadistic flirt, scorning 'so many men' on account of her 'vanity.' So, if the poet intended this passage as a jab at *his* Maryla, what does it say, except that he blames her for *scorning him*. If we're looking for any evidence for the autobiographical roots of *Ballads and Romances*, perhaps we find it here, most clearly. If this bit of psychological criticism is correct, here the poet, whether he intends to or not, exposes a twinge of real jealousy, that of a real man, for a real woman.

Another bit of evidence for the autobiographical basis of the collection might be provided by the poem 'The Glove' [Rękawica], a translation of Schiller's 'Der Handschuh' (1797).[23] It is certainly significant that the one verse he chooses to translate has as its subject a lover fed up with the cruel triviality of woman 'culled from Adam's side [*nomen omen!*] / not to punish him, but rather to delight' ('This I Like'). Having literally ventured among ferocious beasts to fulfil the whim of his flighty lover, Sir Emrod calmly returns from the arena and retakes his seat at her side:

> His lover greets him with joyous embrace,
> And Emrod... flings the glove into her face:
> 'My vow fulfilled, I leave you now, Madame.'
> And off he goes, thinking *Such love be damned!*

---

22 Walc, p. 57.

23 One frequently speaks of Mickiewicz's affinity for Goethe, and their meeting (at which the elder poet presented the younger with the gift of a silver pen). In his article on Mickiewicz's translation of 'The Glove,' Leszek Libera quotes an interesting letter of the poet's, in which Mickiewicz confesses to his friend, classical scholar and translator Józef Jeżowski, 'Nota bene: for a long time now, Schiller has been my unique and most pleasant reading' [*Nb. Szyler jest od dawna moją jedyną i najmilszą lekturą*]. Letter from 11/23 June 1820. Cited in Leszek Libera, 'Mickiewicz als Übersetzer des Schillerschen "Handschuhs"' [Mickiewicz as Translator of Schiller's 'Glove'], *Zeitschrift für Slavische Philologie*, Vol. 47, No. 2 (1987), p. 292.

This is Schiller's poem, but that fact just makes it all the more telling in this context, for casual translators of verse, such as Mickiewicz, do not choose the originals they translate for monetary gain, i.e. on the basis of commission, but rather because the poems resonate with them. So, to choose this poem and to include it in this collection so full of references to his unreciprocated love for Maryla, is significant indeed![24]

Generally speaking, though, whether he was trying to jab her conscience with repeated sardonic pin-pricks or not, the tone of his accusations is generally light-hearted, almost humorous at times. For example, in 'Maryla's Mound' [Kurhanek Maryli]:

> Ask the whole village round
> And everyone's sure to give
> The same answer. Maryla lived
> In that hut; now, in that mound
> She rests.

Even if we were to continue with our psychological criticism, and suggest that the poet is intimating here (vengefully) that Maryla is 'dead to him,' it's hard not to see the black humour here: the first time 'Maryla' is extensively dealt with in this collection, she is in her grave!

Indeed, the poem ends in the same comic fashion. The last stanza is given over to a description of the stranger, who had been listening to the girl's account of Maryla's sad fate, and then, hidden, heard for himself the laments of her lover, her mother, and her girlfriend:

> All this he chanced to hear
> The stranger, and heartsick,
> Wiping away a tear
> Left, with his walking stick.

---

24 According to Leszek Libera, as 'ein braver Zögling eines klassischen Schulsystems' [A fine pupil of a classical school system], Mickiewicz had both a solid practical acquaintance with and a healthy respect for the art of translation. While Libera suggests that his translation from Schiller may have been part of his desire to master the German language, the fact still remains that he was attracted to *this* poem, that *it* spoke to him so strongly, that he wished to recreate it in Polish. See Libera, p. 290.

Before I get to the point here, we must first point out that the motif of the eavesdropper plays a significant role in literature, and an especially moving one in the greatest poem in the Czech language: Karel Hynek Mácha's narrative poem *Máj* [May, 1836].[25] This romantic narrative, with elements of both Byron (the great-souled loner), Schiller (the noble bandit) and Mickiewicz (the element of supernature)[26] revolves around the young bandit Vilém, who, chased from his home during his youth by an unnatural father, becomes a Robin Hood character in the woodlands of Bohemia. When his young love is seduced (or raped) by (what a Romantic coincidence!) that same unnatural father, and Vilém murders him in revenge... Well, to make a long story short, as Gothic/Romantic as the poem sounds, *Máj* is a philosophically deep study of a representative of humanity, alone in his cell on the last night of his life (he is to be executed for his crime on the morrow), reflecting on the excruciatingly cruel situation of mankind: all of us are condemned to death, and none of us, really, knows what lies beyond, if anything. In Part II of the poem, Vilém, 'half sitting and half kneeling' (a position itself indicative of uncertainty in the face of eternal questions), spends some agonising hours meditating on his life and coming death. At a certain point, the turnkey in the room outside his cell hears some clatter therein, and goes in to check on the prisoner. He finds him there catatonic, staring off into space... but his lips are moving, and the turnkey bends his ear close to those lips to catch what Vilém is whispering. Masterfully, Mácha does not report the whispered words:

> Leč strážný nepohnutě stojí,
> Po tváři se mu slzy rojí,
> Ve srdci jeho strašný žal.

---

25 We began our essay with a reference to Mickiewicz's influence on Slovak literature; he had just as great an influence on the Czech Romantics during the period of the *národní obrození* [national revival] of the first half of the nineteenth century, especially, as noted, on Mácha. Skvor's article presents a good thumbnail discussion of his influence on the great poets of the Czech 'national revival,' including, besides Mácha and Erben (see below), František Ladislav Čelakovský, who brought out two important collections of Czech ballads, and translations of Russian ballads. Skvor, p. 170 ff.

26 Justly and convincingly, Skvor compares this most crucial scene in *Máj* to the early musings of Mickiewicz's imprisoned Gustaw-Konrad, in the early scenes of *Forefathers' Eve*, Part III. See Skvor, pp. 172-175.

— Dlouho tak stojí přimražen,
Až sebrav sílu kvapně vstal,
A rychlým krokem spěchá ven.
On sice — dokud ještě žil —
Co slyšel nikdy nezjevil,
Než na vždy bledá jeho líce
Neusmála se nikdy více.²⁷

[But the turnkey stands there, unmoving / And tears are rolling down his cheeks, / A horrid sorrow in his heart. / — Long he stood there, as if frozen, / Until, tensing his strength he stood back up quickly / And left the room at a swift pace. / And indeed — as long as he still lived — What he heard, he never revealed, / Nor on his pale face / Was a smile ever more to be seen].

What did he hear? We will never know. But so profound it was, so profoundly moving or sorrowful, that he could never put it into words, and it changed his life forever. Compare this to what happens in the above cited conclusion to 'Maryla's Mound!' The stranger 'wipes away a tear,' it is true, but then gets up and 'leaves, with his walking stick.' Say what you wish — again, according to a psychological reading of these lines — about the eloquence of 'rejoining the herd' after the catharsis of mourning has run its course, of getting over a heartbreak and 'moving on,' this way of ending one of the more artfully constructed poems found in the collection (more of this later) is anticlimactic, to say the least. *What? He picks up his stick and moves on? Just like that? Shrugging at such a tragedy?* one imagines the unflattered Maryla reacting to this. She'd much rather see a life-changing event here, as in the case of Mácha's turnkey, and instead she gets... a shrug? An 'oh, well...'? *Well, what else was he supposed to do?* we hear Mickiewicz respond in our imagination. *Beat a fourth road to the tomb?* Here too, jab or not, Mickiewicz defuses the pathos of a scene that he might have handled very differently.

If there is an autobiographical element to *Ballads and Romances*, the striking thing is the manner in which it oscillates between studied, if irritated, unconcern, humour, and heartfelt blame. In considering his summertime

---

27   Karel Hynek Mácha, *Máj* [May] II: 219-228, in *Spisy, Díl první* [Writings. Vol. 1] (Praha: Nákladem knihkupectví I.L. Kober, 1862).

fling with 'Maryla,' the poet, winter-bound in loneliness, reflects thus in 'To my Friends' [Do Przyjaciół], the poem that fronts 'This I Like:'

> He who with camel-hair brush and oil would slay time,
>   Let him paint her, and out-sublime art;
> But the bard? Let him capture in immortal rhyme
>   Her intelligence, virtue, and heart.
>
> As for me — although all that is fresh to my mind
>   It is solace I seek here, not fame;
> And so if I am able, I'll tell you this time
>   Of my late springtime, heartbroken game.

He will not be that 'bard;' she'll need another poet to 'immortalise' her virtues, etc., in his work; he, meanwhile, will spend his time drawing up a charge-sheet:

> Maryla found terms of endearment... a chore.
>   She dispensed them in tittle and drip.
> She'd hear *I love you!* hundreds of times, or more,
>   But *I like you* she'd never let slip...

Studied unconcern, blame, and (as we have seen and are about to see again), bitter humour characterise the poet's expression of the Adam/Maryla myth to which this very collection gave rise. In other words, whatever autobiographical material may be at the bottom of *Ballads and Romances*, it is not merely confessional verse; artistic skill predominates — the careful hand of the talented craftsman is to be found in every stanza of the poems here collected.

One of the more visible proofs of poetic craftsmanship — and comic as well — is the motif of tantalisation that appears at least twice in these poems. For example, towards the end of the narrator's interview with the spectre of Maryla in 'This I Like,' the latter declares:

> 'I'm grateful! And now this is granted me,
>   To part the clouds, show you your future road.
> You shall know a Maryla, too, but she...'
>   At this — alas! — The dawn's first rooster crowed.

You can almost see Maryla leaning forward in her chair, pricking her ears at the ellipses... only to have her hopes dashed, as the rooster crows and the spectre vanishes to heavenly glory, leaving her story untold, her glory undocumented for generations present and future. In other words, we're tempted to say that, just as Maryla tantalised him during life, so here Mickiewicz tantalises Maryla (and the reader). He does this again in 'The Minstrel' [Dudarz]. There, the eponymous minstrel, relating the story of the death of the unrequited lover to the crowd listening to his ballad, repeats the lover's last words. As he dies, he breaks off her name, just as it was about to leave his lips:

> "'If she invites you near the cheery flame
> Of her hearth... tell —" but then, alas!
> He faded, with the Virgin's name
> Upon his lips, but only the first half...'

Of course, we are being cruelly unfair to the historical Maryla to see in her a vain, cruel beauty, whose flightiness is stymied (and good for her! take that!) by the poet, just as she was about to be flattered by becoming the heroine of a romantic narrative, or at least identified by name as such. But that is the game that Mickiewicz (again, justly or unjustly) invites us to play.

For all its sly pathos, this passage should also be pointed out as an example of Mickiewicz's poetic craft. The dying man, obviously, says the first syllable of Maryla's name, 'Ma—,' which the minstrel, not privy to the story of his heartbreak (as the sad man never went into details), takes rather to be the first syllable of 'Mary,' the name of the Mother of God, Help of Sinners, to whom the dying man has recourse, begging her, as the second verse of the Ave has it, to 'pray for him... at the hour of his death.' Those classically-trained detractors of Mickiewicz, like it or not, simply couldn't begrudge him their approval at this passage, which displays the poet's familiarity with a frequent trait of classical tragedy: the oracle misunderstood. The 'truth' has been, as it were, blown out of the Sybil's cave at the opening of the leather flap, but while the petitioner holds it in his hands, having raced about collecting the leaves upon which it is written, now he must put it back together. And when he does, he gets it wrong... As does the murderous wife in 'Lilie' [Lilies]. Having slain her husband upon his return from the Kievan expedition of King Bolesław the Bold, fearing the discovery of her infidelities committed during his absence, the frantic woman hastens off to a nearby hermit. She confesses what she's done, but does not receive absolution. Instead:

> 'O, woman!' says the old hermit,
> 'It's not in sorrow for blood spilt
> That you come here? It's not regret,
> But fear of censure for your guilt?
> If so, be off now — go in peace.
> Throw off your care, make bright your face;
> Your secret's safe, and for all time.
> Such is the nature of your crime:
> What you have done, no others know
> Save your husband. He's dead, and so
> No one can call you to account
> But he — and he's deep underground.'

More evidence of Mickiewicz's erudition for those classicists who 'assume that there can be nothing deserving of praise in Romanticism.' For the hermit here is not just a Catholic priest, who cannot absolve even an honest sinner if she be not truly penitent, but — again — the classical type of tragic oracle who delivers a truth to the petitioner, but one that is entirely misunderstood. The woman feels safe — *no one can give me up except my husband deep underground*, believing that to be impossible, whereas just the opposite will happen. Just as she transgressed the commandments of God in murdering her husband, here she doubts in His justice and miraculous power. That very thing she feels is impossible will happen, and she will stand convicted on the evidence of this 'Pietrowin' (another reference that those 'wisemen' with eye and magnifying glass would certainly recognise).[28]

With these references to the breadth of poetic imagination and aptitude displayed by Mickiewicz in *Ballads and Romances*, it might be good to say a few words here concerning

---

28   A miraculous legend first mentioned in the eleventh century *Life of St Stanisław*, written by the hagiographer Wincenty z Kielczy, according to which the patron of Poland, St Stanisław, the Archbishop of Kraków, resurrected Piotr Strzemieńczyk, summoning him to give testimony in court in a case of a disputed transfer of lands.

MICKIEWICZ'S POETIC VERSATILITY.

As a title collection of 'ballads' and 'romances' composed in the third decade of the nineteenth century, the poems that make up Mickiewicz's first embarkation upon the deep waters of literature tack close to traditional forms. The poems are generally built up from quatrains in tetrameter, sometimes with lines alternating tetrameter/trimeter, sometimes with the lines lengthening into the traditionally classic Polish lines of eleven or thirteen syllables. The lines rhyme without exception. Generally speaking, the linking of the words in any given stanza is A-B-A-B, with stanzas of A-B-B-A occurring here and there, without any deep sense to the variations, indulged in, perhaps, only for reasons mechanical — the flow of the narrative led to more convenient rhymes this way than in the general alternating pattern.

But there is no slavish uniformity here. Although he doesn't approach the mastery of, say, Thomas Hardy in English, who hardly ever uses the same metre twice, to say nothing of the experiments, to remain in England, of so careful a stylist as Gerard Manley Hopkins (nor should we even expect such of him), still, in *Ballads and Romances*, Mickiewicz shows himself to be not only conscious of varied poetic form, but skilled at it. Even though those lines of 'The Three Budryses' [Trzech Budrysów] written in poulter's measure might fall jarringly on the contemporary ear, the manner in which he preserves a natural narrative flow while sustaining internal rhymes in lines one and three of each stanza is impressive.

'Romanticism' is justly an immortal poem, not only for its significance as the clarion-call of the new movement in literature and culture, but also on account of its very contemporary feel. The marvellous manner in which Mickiewicz varies his stanzaic forms and line lengths in that poem lend it a freshness that, I am convinced, will never stale. It certainly hasn't yet, and two hundred years have passed.

In this manner too, the sparse, tight, lean lines of his translation 'The Glove' are a virtuoso showpiece. This is due, of course, more to the fashions of Weimar Classicism, and Neoclassicism in general, than to any idiosyncratic poetic experimentation. And yet, here too, it's almost as if Mickiewicz — familiar with such sprightly turns-on-a-dime from the classical fables of Ignacy Krasicki, for example — were saying to his classicist critics: 'See? Anything you can do, I can do better...'

And then there is the surprising, Biblical diction in which much of the lamenting of Maryla's loved ones are cached in 'Maryla's Mound.' Her young lover, about to march off to a welcome death fighting in Russia, spurning the material benefits that would redound to him upon marrying someone else, exclaims:

> Blight take the seed! Rust scald the leaves!
> Let all the unmilled grain must and rot;
> Let the neighbours filch my sheaves!
> No longer shall I drive
> Wolf from the sheep-fold; what for?
> Maryla is no more!

Similarly, her mother expresses herself in Old Testament-like ardour, a bit more calm and elegiac, but just as engaging in the manner in which form encompasses and further develops feelings of loss and desolation:

> But now, my daughter, now you're gone!
> Our home is like a desert waste.
> Whoever draws near, passes on;
> Door-hinges unrevolving, rust in place;
> With moss our flagstone pathway's overgrown.
> Both man and God now shun our vacant home,
> Maryla, Daughter! Now you're gone!

Thus, poetically speaking, Mickiewicz's *Ballads and Romances* is a complex composition. It showcases various strands of the nascent Romantic tradition, along with the erotic themes discussed above, and the importance of supernature; we also find a typical romantic interest in folk tales, folk etymologies (why, for example, bitter-bur is known as *car* [Tsar] in the regions around Lake Świteź), and exoticism — Lithuanian and Ukrainian themes, for instance. These were exotic enough for the inhabitants of Warsaw, Kraków, and Wrocław, to say nothing of the truly Eastern themes, like that of the 'Turkish Ballad' entitled 'The Renegade' [Renegat].

The dim Slavic past is also referenced — similarly a favourite interest of the cultural nationalists à la Herder in the Romantic Age. In 'The Three Budryses,' the Lithuanian heroes are set apart from Russians, Poles and Germans by their stubborn devotion to paganism (they were the last of the Northern European peoples to be baptised), but even more, in 'Tukaj,' when the eponymous hero is summoned from his sickbed for a mystical journey to the top of Mount Żanowa; there he is challenged by a mysterious old man called 'Polel' — the supposed name of an ancient pagan Slavic deity.'[29]

Indeed, it's not all sighing and weeping in *Ballads and Romances*; it's not even all Romanticism. The humorous verse 'Mrs Twardowska' [Pani Twardowska], gives a comic twist, macaronisms and all, to the Faustus/Twardowski[30] myth which is much more similar to the wit of the age of Voltaire than the deadly serious theology of Christopher Marlowe:

> All is prepared. Twardowski leaps
>   Upon the horse, he trots and canters,
> Meanwhile the devil hammers heaps
>   Of beard and seed. Twardowski banters:
>
> 'I am impressed, upon my soul!
>   My second wish is a bit stricter:
> Come, take a bath now in this bowl
>   Brim-full of *aqua benedicta*.'
>
> The devil gives a little yelp.
>   He pales and shrinks and starts to sweat,
> But the command given, there's no help
>   For it — and so he seethes and frets
>
> Up to his neck in woe. Then he
>   Leaps out, sore, scalded, but he's won!

---

29 The anthropologist and mythologist Aleksander Brückner challenges this common identification, suggesting instead that the words 'Lel' and 'Polel' were not proper names, but rather meaningless rhythmical interjections in the choruses of folk ballads. Whatever the case may be, such an identification, even if mistaken, was current during Mickiewicz's time. For more information, see Aleksander Brückner, *Mitologia słowiańska i polska* [Slavic and Polish Mythology] (Warsaw: PWN, 1985).

30 Twardowski was supposedly a sixteenth-century noble from Kraków, of whom it was said (as it was of the historical character of Johann Faust [1480–1540], a former student of alchemy at the University of Kraków), that he sold his soul to the devil for magical powers. Unlike Faust, however, Twardowski outwitted the devil, and legend has him now far from the grip of Hell, on the moon.

> 'The jig is up! And now, to me
> Your soul is forfeit. Let's go! Come!'

The above-mentioned 'Tukaj' is also a Faustian tale, complete with an appearance by Mephistophiles. But, while there is comedy in 'Tukaj' too, it offers a deeper message about love between us, here and now. Asked to choose a person he trusts as completely as himself (as part of a plot to gain immortal life), Tukaj:

> 'Yes...' he says, and hesitates,
> Then, bites his lips, and wrings his hands,
> 'Yes, yes. My wife. Our wedding bands...'
> And he believes, and yet he fears.
> A blush upon his cheeks appears;
> Ashamed, he wavers, wrings his hands.
> He's thought it through. His answer is —
> Nothing. Abashed, silent he stands.
> 'So, die! You dare to make demands?
> You trust no one, it so appears —
> Is it so bitter, then, to die?'

The message to us here is too patent to need elaboration. But now, we seem to have come full circle. Love, fidelity, and the need for both true love and dependable fidelity to withstand the challenges of this life, and even the grave, return us, like it or not, to

MARYLA, MARYLA, AND ONCE AGAIN MARYLA.

Of the four verses not included in the original 1822 edition of *Ballads and Romances*, but appended to the 1852 Brockhaus edition, most worthy of note is the ballad 'The Escape' [Ucieczka]. Mickiewicz's 'Lenore,' it is the most expansive, and daring, expression of the rights of love to be found in the poetry of the great romantic.

We have already seen how Mickiewicz presents the otherworld as an inevitable extension of this present plane of existence, and revenant spirits not as necessarily evil, but — potentially — blessed, if temporarily suffering, emissaries of God, sent to us with messages intended to help us on the hazard-strewn path to our home in Heaven. In Slavic countries, revenant spirits tend to be benign, not ghoulish³¹ — whether this be because of a Catholic understanding of the cosmos and eschatology, in contrast to that found in Protestant nations like Great Britain and its offspring America, or due to the familiarity with and acceptance of the processes of life, including death, found among traditional, agricultural societies in contrast to the antiseptic modern urban world, where all that is unpleasant is hidden from our eyes or delegated to others. In the case of 'The Escape,' however, the situation is different, and the spirit more in line with familiar, threatening revenant lovers of the 'Lenore' type, the most famous example of which is the 1773 Gothic narrative of Gottfried August Bürger.³²

'The Escape' has all the elements of the Gothic romance. A young Maiden, whose lover has been off warring for more than a year, is in desperate straits. 'Her charms wasting,' while she pines for her intended, whom she (and everyone else) assumes is no longer coming back, she finds herself being herded towards marriage by the prince (her intended groom), her mother, and the local priest. Cornered, she has recourse to a local wise woman and, through black magic — she abjures priest and Christianity in a vivid scene of spell-casting — she summons her dead lover, who visits her at night, spends some pleasant hours in loving conversation by her bedside, and then invites her to join him 'forever' in his 'castle.'

As they race on through the night, spectre and spectral horse straining to arrive at the graveyard before the cock crows, at which — presumably — they would vanish, and the maiden would be rescued from the yawning maw of the tomb, we learn that various objects of personal devotion that the Maiden carries about with her impede their progress:

> 'O lover mine, rein in the steed!
> He's spooked, and so he's gone astray —
> So many trees lie thwart the way
> I'm knocked against them; scratched, I bleed!'
> 'My darling, what's that string I see

---

31   I argue that this is at the basis of most Slovak folk poetry dealing with revenant spirits. See Charles S. Kraszewski, 'Revenant Spirits in Slovak Folk Narrative Poems,' *Kosmas*, Vol. 20, No. 2 (2007), pp. 1-27.

32   In his essay on Romantic poetry, Mickiewicz explicitly singles out Bürger's 'Lenore' as an epochal publication that opened the floodgates to the ballad form in Germany and England. See Mickiewicz, 'O poezji romantycznej,' p. 90.

> That dangles from your pocket there?'
> 'My lover, that's my rosary.
> The other is my scapular.'
>
> 'O, the damned necklace! Cast it wide
> Away! It blinds the charger's eyes!
> See how he shivers, shunts aside —
> Throw it away!' As off it flies,
> Terror removed, see how the charger
> Surges a full five miles farther.

One would think that the good, pious girl (who has, all the same, indulged in the black arts!) ought to know that all is not right here. If the spirit conducting her to his 'castle' were a good man, or a blessed spirit, he would not be upset at her devotionalia. Why does she throw away prayer book, rosary, scapular, and gold cross, immediately she is commanded to by the bitter rider? Is she not aware of what she is doing?

That is just the point. *She is*. In his 'Maiden,' Mickiewicz is presenting us with an extreme ideal of love: one that not only laughs in the face of death, but one that risks salvation itself in order to remain true. Just as in the Great Improvisation scene in *Forefathers' Eve*, Part III, in which Mickiewicz's greatest hero, Konrad, pulls up short of blasphemy, here too the poet halts at the edge of approving this behaviour. Yet in his constant refrain 'Maiden, Maiden, have you no fear?' we have no shocked admonition of the sinful girl, but rather an awestruck wonder at a love so great.

To put this in a proper context, let us consider first another ballad, Karel Jaromír Erben's 'Svatební košile' [Wedding Shirts, 1853],[33] which owes much to both Bürger's ballad, and Mickiewicz's.[34] At the climax of this poem, the orphaned girl recognises who her 'lover' is — at the very lip of the grave. Falling to her knees in horror, she calls upon the Virgin Mary in prayer:

---

33   Collected in *Kytice* [A Bouquet], following *Máj*, the most beloved verse collection of the Czech nineteenth century. We cite here Karel Jaromír Erben, *Kytice z básní* [A Bouquet from the Poems (of KJE)] (Praha: Jaroslav Pospíšil, 1861).

34   Skvor, pp. 176-177. According to him, the influence of Mickiewicz's ballads can be found throughout *Kytice*.

> Maria panno! při mně stůj,
> U syna svého oroduj!
> Nehodně jsem tě prosila:
> Ach odpust, co jsem zhřešila!
> Maria, matko milosti!
> Z té moci zlé mne vyprosti.
>
> [Mary, dear Virgin! Stand by me, / Pray to your Son on my behalf! / I was wrong to ask you for such a thing: / Oh, forgive me for so sinning! Mary, mother of grace! / Beg for me rescue from this evil power].

And indeed, at that moment, the cock crows, and the girl is saved. It is a very moral story, befitting the Biedermeier period; virtue wins out in the end. The Virgin Mary, like a wise mother, allowed the game to continue so far — in order to teach the rebellious child a lesson — and then pulled her, literally, out of the fire at the very moment the lesson was learned. As for Mickiewicz's heroine, her end is different indeed:

> The cross fell to the earth. Soon after,
> The rider threw his arms about
> The maiden — fire burst from his mouth
> And eye-sockets, and human laughter
> Erupted from the horse, who flew
> Over the walls as the cock crew
> And the bells rang for morning Mass.
> On his way there, the rector passed
> The graveyard — nowhere to be found
> Horse, rider, Maiden — all around
> Was quiet, but in the lifting gloom
> He saw — one fresh and crossless tomb.

Is this a tragedy, or a victory? Does love lead the Maiden to her destruction, or is an eternity, even if in Hell, with her beloved, preferable to her over Heavenly glory without him? As we say above, Mickiewicz never goes so far as to suggest that. But in his 'Maiden, Maiden, have you no fear?' his awe at her courage, however misguided it may be, is obvious.

Nor is this the end of the story. The priest's reaction to the story he pieces together from the evidence is significant. The last two verses of the poem read: 'Long mused he, while the matins tolled, / That day, he said Mass for two souls.' You don't say Masses, or pray, for the damned souls in Hell. The priest's reaction shows a recognition on his part that, whatever the two — spectre and Maiden — may have done, they were motivated by true love, and that may be salvific. He at least entertains the possibility that they may be in Purgatory, not Hell — and the Mass he says is a concrete recognition of the fact that true love must never be interfered with, by matchmaker, mother, or clergyman. Whether or not they knew that her lover was dead, they had no right to force her to abandon her devotion to him, harrying her on to a wedding she despised. The Mass he says is partial penance for his own role in the events that pushed her on to her decision. As so often in the case of the *Ballads and Romances* of Adam Mickiewicz — message (from the beyond) received.

ACKNOWLEDGEMENTS

It is always a great pleasure to recreate, however feebly, the works of Adam Mickiewicz. I am indebted to the Polish Cultural Institute, London, for entrusting to me the translation of *Ballads and Romances* as a part of the two hundredth anniversary celebration of their original publication. I also express my deep gratitude to Glagoslav Publications, for their continued support of the Polish classics in English.

Olu, moja kochana, jak wiesz... jak zawsze...

Banská Štiavnica
26 November 2021

Ballads and Romances

(Wilno, 1822)

THE PRIMROSE[35]

As the earliest song fills the skies,
   As the earliest morning lark flies,
The primrose blinks open her eyes,
   Where beneath a gold sunshade she lies.

I

Too early, dear flower, for still
   The midnight frosts creep near to you,
Snow blankets yet summit and hill,
   And the oak-glade is dripping with dew.

Dear primrose, O dim your sweet light!
   'Neath the cloak of your mother come, curl —
For the frost's tooth seeks something to bite;
   Illness lurks in the dew's shining pearl!

THE FLOWER

Like the butterfly's, our days flit past:
   At dawn, life sings, at noon — hear death call.
Better one hour in spring, while it lasts,
   Than whole weeks of Decembers in fall.

If you're seeking an offering rare
   For the gods, or some love divine,
Plait a wreath from the blossoms I bear —
   No more lovely a chaplet you'll twine.

I

You bloom and grow, O primrose mine,
   In base grass, wild woods are your haunts;
Small of size, none too brightly you shine —
   Whence the boldness in all of your vaunts?

---

35   Primula veris.

You neither sparkle like the dawn,
   Nor have you the tulip's crest;
You've neither lily's splendid gown
   Nor the chaste rose's blushing breast.

Into a wreath I'll plait you now,
   But whence this brash self-confidence?
Will my love set you on her brow?
   Will you be lauded by my friends?

THE FLOWER

With me your friends won't be dismayed,
   The angel of the early spring.
Friendship, like me, prefers the shade
   To flash and pomp and garish things.

Am I worthy your sweetheart? Say,
   What do you think, Marylka, dear?
When he gave you a primrose spray
   You paid him back… with his first tears!

ROMANTICISM

Methinks I see... where?
— In my mind's eye.
Shakespeare

Listen, girlie! Hey!
— She doesn't hear —
This is your village! It's bright day!
Around you not a living soul is near.
What would you clasp? There's nothing there at all!
Who are you speaking to? Whom do you call?
— She doesn't hear —

    Now like a stone she stands,
    Casting on neither hand
    Her glance, and now she spins to face
    What? And bursting into tears,
    She seems to crush something in her embrace,
    Sobbing and smiling from ear to ear.

'It's you, Jasieńko, in the night!
Ah, even dead you hold me dear!
Come closer, closer! It's all right,
But, shh! So Stepmother won't hear!

'Ah, let her hear! ...Now that you're gone,
You're dead and buried, life goes on,
They say — You're dead, Jasieńko! And I'm scared!
But if it's you, I'm frightened? Why?
It's you! That same cheek, that same eye —
That same white shirt you wear!

'And you — white as a sheet as well,
And cold... How cold the hands I grip!
Come, I'll press you to my breast a spell,
And hold you tight — lip to lip!

'Ah, how cold it must be in the tomb —
Take me! I'll die with you right here!
Since you died, it's been two long years...
I hate this world of gloom

'Where I'm surrounded on all hands
By evil folk, who mock and jeer —
I speak, and no one understands.
No one can see what I see, clear!

'Come in the day sometimes... I'm dreaming? No!
No, no... I hold your hands in mine...
Jasieńko, wait! Come back! Don't go!
It's still early. Early! We've lots of time!

'My God! I hear the rooster crowing,
The dawn shatters the windowpane...
Jasieńko, stay! Where are you going?
He's gone! And here, wretch, I remain!'

Still the girl would her love caress,
She races after, cries, and stumbles to the ground.
Seeing her fall, at her sobs of distress,
The crowd of villagers gathers round.

'Let's pray!' the simple people cry,
'Jasieńko's soul must have come by
To visit his intended bride
Whom he loved so, before he died!'

I hear them, and I too believe.
I pray with them, and I too grieve.

    Then, 'Listen, girlie!' I hear someone shout,
    'You simpletons! She's raving, the poor lass!
    Here, trust *my* eye, and this my looking glass!
    There's no such thing as ghosts that flit about!

'Spirits are but the stuff of old wives' tales
Brewed in the vat of ignorant dreaming.
That girl is babbling nonsense!' so he rails,
'And you, against pure reason are blaspheming!'

'The child feels,' I answer humbly. 'Truly,
Those simple people have great faith and hope.
Feeling and faith speak more profoundly to me
Than wise-man's eye and ground-glass microscope.

'You know dead truths, as you dissect and sunder
Planets to atoms, stars to sparks; your art
Grasps no live truth. You'll never glimpse a wonder
Unless you feel, and gaze into the heart!'

ŚWITEŹ
(A BALLAD)

TO MICHAŁ WERESZCZAKA

If ever you toward Nowogród should ride,
   And err about Płużyny's gloomy brake,
Make sure to pull your frothy steed aside,
   To pause a spell beside the pristine lake.

Yes, there you'll find Lake Świteź' brilliant breast,
   Which like a circle of great ambit lies,
Ringed thickly round about by dark forest;
   So smooth its surface, like a pane of ice.

Now, should you wander close on a clear night
   To gaze upon the lake, your eye shall meet
Two moons, two starfields — one above you, bright,
   Another, there, glittering at your feet.

Unsure what lies before your mount, you'll halt —
   Checking your steed by jerking at the reins:
Have you reached the world's end, where Heaven's vault
   Curls down to kiss those glassy, star-flecked plains?

In vain you seek to grip with panicked eye
   The solid shore — you clutch and still you miss;
You seem to hang suspended in the sky
   Weightless, in some cerulean abyss.

Thus, when the weather's calm, and stars are bright,
   It's pleasant to deceive one's eye, I'm told.
Yet he who visits Lake Świteź at night
   Must have a heart that's more than middling bold,

For what dark revels there the devils hold!
   What ghosts and spectres shriek throughout the night!

To hear the old folks' tales, my blood runs cold,
   And till the blessed dawn I quake in fright.

Sometimes the lake's aflame; thick billows rise
   Of smoke — it seems as if a city swarms
Within: and quarrels, shouts, and women's cries,
   Bells frenzied peal, amidst the clash of arms.

Then — sudden calm; the firestorm disappears
   And nothing but fir-sighing fills the air.
Deep, muffled voices is all that one hears;
   That, and a girl — sobbing a mournful prayer.

What does it mean? There are as many tales
   As there are tongues. And no one's been below
The water's surface: there the reason fails
   To plumb the truth. The meaning? Who should know?

The local lord, of ancient family,
   To whom the region round the lake belonged,
Determined once to solve the mystery.
   He sought advice, and cogitated long,

Then ordered sounding-gear and built a fleet
   Of trawler, barge, and hollowed-pine canoe
To dredge the lake a full two hundred feet,
   Spending a fair pile before he was through!

'Who starts with God ends well,' I said to him;
   'Seek the Lord's aid at such a weighty pass.'
And so he sent for the priest from Cyryn,
   And at the local parish bought a Mass.

Then, vested in his alb, the priest asperges
   The men, the task, blessing them from the shore;
The lord says 'Go!' and the flotilla surges
   Out on the lake; the seine sinks with a roar.

It seeks so deep it pulls the bobbers down
   Along with it, so deep the lake must be!
The cables strain and creak, while sinkers sound
   The depths no human eye will ever see.

Then from the shore they close the purse-seine tight;
   The fishers tense their muscles as they heave.
So, what lake monster was pulled into sight?
   I'll tell you — though I think you'll scarce believe...

You see, there was no monster there. Instead
   There was... a living woman in the net.
Her face shone bright, her lips were coral-red,
   Her tawny locks were long and dripping wet.

She heads for shore. Some, rooted to the place
   Stand, paralysed with fear, while others seek
Safety in scampering. Away they race...!
   But gentle are the words they hear her speak.

'Young men, you know that with impunity
   Till now no one has set forth from this shore —
These depths are filled with those who thoughtlessly
   Sailed forth, never to be seen any more.

'So you, bold fellow, with your haughty friends
   Would have won watery graves for all your pains,
But that this land is your inheritance,
   And that our blood is flowing in your veins...

'Though worth stripes is vain curiosity,
   Because you sought God's aid ere coming here,
God's aid you'll have, for now He speaks through me,
   Revealing all the secrets of this mere.

'This lake, that bitter-bur and reeds surround,
   The pane of which you marred with flailing oar,

Was once a populous and a mighty town —
   That now lies deep beneath its sandy floor.

'A city vibrant, rich, renowned in arms —
   Just like this lake, Świteź the town was named.
Stout were its men, its women of great charms,
   Beneath Prince Tuhan's rule it waxed in fame.

'Vistas unsullied by that gloomy wood:
   As far as one could see bobbed fields of wheat
From here to the high walls of Nowogród,
   Old Lithuania's fair ducal seat.

''Twas there that, suddenly, the armed might
   Of Russia pounced, with no one to defend her
Save Mendog — all our nation quailed in fright —
   Surrounded, must brave Mendog now surrender?

'He sent out urgent pleas to his allies —
   To my father, Tuhan, before all others:
"Our capital's fate in your power lies,
   Tuhan! Come, quick, and come with all your brothers!"

'No sooner had he scanned the message than
   Tuhan commenced assembling an armed force.
Soon rallied to his call five thousand men,
   Bravely arrayed in heavy arms, and horsed.

'The trumpets blare, the youths cheer, setting out
   Like thunder, pennants fluttering… but then,
Tuhan halts, wavers, gripped it seems with doubt
   And soon he's back in his own halls again!

'He turns to me: "Must the inhabitants
   Of my town perish, while I'm serving lords
Of other lands? You have no battlements
   Save these our bucklers, breasts, and these our swords.

"'If I were to divide this meagre might,
   I couldn't help defend my brothers' lives;
But should I throw them all into that fight,
   What fate awaits our daughters and our wives?"

"'Father,' I cried, "untimely is this fright —
   Go now! And lead your men where glory calls!
God is our fortress. In a dream last night
   I saw his angel soar above these walls!

"'Around Świteź his sword flares, bright and clear;
   Upon the walls his pennons rest. He sings:
As long as Tuhan's men war far from here,
   Świteź shall nestle safe beneath my wings."

'So Tuhan, heartened, raced back to his force
   And rushed to war. But when the deep night fell,
A moil of noise grew near — swords clashing, horse
   Pummelling the sod — and horrid shrieks, and yells!

'Rams batter — gates fall, one after another.
   From black skies darts hail down, thick, deadly, wild;
In panic stumble old man, frenzied mother,
   Defenceless maiden and innocent child

'Into the keep, wailing "Help! Bar the door!
   The Russians — at our heels with iron and flame!
If die we must, let's take our own lives, for
   Death, although fierce, will rescue us from shame!"

'Then, suddenly, rage takes the place of fear.
   Sacked wealth is heaped into a towering pyre,
Torches of flaming pitch are hurried near
   And voices howl in a horrid choir:

"'Damned be he, who virtuous death rejects!"
   I pulled at them, and begged them to relent,

But no — they kneel, all, and bare their necks,
   While overhead sharp battle-axes glint!

'Crime on all hands — shall we accept our fetters
   With meek hands outstretched to the cruel horde?
Or — godless self-slaughter? Would that be better?
   I cry to God: "O Lord above all Lords!

'"If we cannot resist these vicious bands,
   Slay us Thyself! O, may we meet our doom
By lightning hurled down from Thy sacred hands,
   Or swallowed whole, while living, by the tomb!"

'Then — whiteness. Blinding, flashing all around,
   As if the day had chased away the night,
With panicked eyes I scan for solid ground
   Beneath my feet... but nothing meets my sight...!

'Thus we escaped our shaming with our lives.
   In each reed that you see there lives a lass:
All of fair Świteź' daughters, maids and wives,
   You see by God transformed here... into grass.

'Those whitish blooms the lazy ripples stir,
   That bob upon the lake like butterflies
Cupped on leaves, like green needles of the fir
   When the fresh virgin snow upon them lies —

'Immaculate in flesh, thus they endure,
   The image of their chasteness in this rest;
Retaining still their candour, chill and pure,
   No mortal hand shall stain their spotless breast.

'The Tsar and his louts learnt this all too soon
   When, trotting near Świteź, they reined their steeds
To pluck some flowers their helmets to festoon,
   Plaiting bright nosegays, jaunty chaplets, wreaths...

'To find that arms that plunged into the depths
  Withered! So strong the power of those blooms;
An illness — frightful — ending but with death
  Unerringly and swiftly spelt their doom.

'Though ages blur this ancient memory,
  Still, like a teasing echo from afar,
The folk retain, in speech, the history:
  The name they give the bitter-bur is... *tsar*.'

Thus ending, back toward the lake she turns.
  The water buckles, swallows net and barge;
A twisting wind the shrieking forest churns,
  And heavy billows pummel the lake-marge.

The lakebed splits into a fissure grim;
  In vain the eye scans the vast, sandy floor.
For soon the waters swell back to the brim,
  And the lake maiden is seen nevermore.

[1820–1821]

THE ŚWITEZIANKA[36]
(A BALLAD)

Who might be that boy, so lovely and fresh?
And who is that girl by his side?
Slowly they stroll on the banks of Świteź,
In the pale and the ghostly moonlight.

She feeds him raspberries, a basket she bears,
While he binds her a chaplet of flowers.
Certainly lovers, each one's dearest dear,
Arms entwined, they spend the sweet night hours.

Every night you may see them thus walk near the flood;
They meet here at this larch, then they go.
The young boy is a keeper in the nearby wood;
Who's the girl? Well, I really don't know…

Whence comes she? You'd search for the answer in vain.
When she's gone, no one knows where she is.
On the marsh bank she sprouts, a bloom freshened by rain,
And she fades like the will o' the wisp.

'Show me, my lovely, delight of my eyes,
The paths you tread here to my side.
Who are your kin? Show me where your home lies.
Lovers true should have nothing to hide!

'Now the summer is past, and the leaves are all sere;
Soon the autumn rains will start to pour.
Must I always be waiting for you to come, here,
In this wilderness, by the lakeshore?

---

36 It is said that Ondines or water Nymphs appear sometimes on the banks of Lake Świteź; the folk call these *Świezianki*.

'Must you ever glide like timid deer through the grove,
Like a ghost through the thickets at night?
Remain with me, rather, the one whom you love,
And who loves you — remain by my side!

'For my little hut stands in the meadows quite near —
Where abundance of fruit is, and milk.
In the dense forest's clearing, not so far from here,
Where is food and game of every ilk!'

— 'Not so fast, not so fast, O you boldest of boys!
For I mind what my old father said:
The sweetest of songbirds lives in a man's voice,
And the slyest fox dens in his head.

'Is your heart true? Or fickle? I can't help but fear
It may prove just like yon weathervane.
Should I heed your entreaties, my boy, and stay here,
What about you? Will *you* always remain?'

In reply, the boy knelt, the dread powers below
Invoking, to witness his troth;
With a fistful of sand, 'neath the sacred moon's glow...
But — will he keep unbroken his oath?

'Remember, my huntsman, your promise to keep.
Break it not! For the perjurer's role
In this life is to moan and incessantly weep;
In the next — woe to his foul soul!'

And then, having said this, the beauteous maid
Set the chaplet of blooms on her head,
And, sprinting away, from a distance, she bade
Him farewell, fading long past the mead.

In vain did the keeper then rise from his knees,
Speeding off to where — he reckoned — she'd gone...

For she spun and she vanished like mist on the breeze,
Leaving him just as always — alone.

So he turned, in his solitude, once more to wend
His way homeward along the moist track;
Quiet and still it was all through the fen,
Save when trodden dry twigs snapped and cracked.

But his errant feet lead him, musing, back to the lake
Where he glances about in surprise.
Then the wind of a sudden roars through the thick brake
And the waters in foaming swells rise.

Ah, the waves! How they swell and they pound and they thresh
The long grasses, then — wonderful sight!
Above the moon-silvered banks of Lake Świteź
Spurts a maid of great beauty, and bright!

O, her face — like a chaplet weft of the pale rose,
Sprinkled with the pure tears of the dew:
Thin and gauzy, like mists on the breeze, did her clothes
Lightly cover her figure with blue.

'O you beautiful child! So young and so fresh!'
Thus the maiden did tenderly croon —
'Why is it you wander the banks of Świteź
By the light of the pale silver moon?

'Is it for that wispy flirt that your heart's in mourning,
Who tempts you o'er thicket and hill?
For that breath of the mist that you err after, yearning,
Who's laughing, perhaps, at you still?

'Hearken to me, rather, my lonely friend.
Sigh no more, toss off sadness at last!
Come to me, come, and the whole night we'll spend
Dancing over these waters of glass.

'Like the swift-winged swallow, if such is your wish,
Above the waves you'll swoop and you'll skim;
Or, carefree and gaily, like two happy fish,
All the day long together we'll swim.

'Until on the pure silver lakebed at night,
Beneath our tent-canvas of glass,
We shall rest our heads on water-lilies of white
And watch the dreamy gods as they pass.'

Then her breasts she uncovers, like swans they are, white —
The flushed lad drops his eyes, modestly;
And the maiden is near him, as quickly as light
Crying: 'Come now, my sweetheart, to me!'

Then she flies off again, to alight with her feet
On the lake, where she skims, dances, hops
An arc like a rainbow; then playfully beats
Toward the charmed boy, silver water drops.

So the keeper runs close... but he pulls up before
He should plunge... starts... again hesitates...
Then a little blue wavelet creeps up to the shore,
Licks his feet... kisses them... titillates...

And keeps on caressing him, tempting him on,
So his heart melts as on the wave pets,
Like a bold lover secretly tickling his palm.
Soon, the shy wispy girl he forgets!

O, his troth to his sweetheart the keeper forgets
And his sacred vow holds in despite;
All too blindly he rushes into the lake's depths
In pursuit of new tempting delight.

Yes, he runs and he searches, he searches and runs,
His new ardour excited to slake;

All too soon from the shallows he boldly swims on —
Plashing in the deep heart of the lake.

Soon enough in his hand her palm snowy he feels,
His eyes fix on her beautiful face;
She darts playfully from him, he ardently reels
To press his lips to hers... On they race!

Then a sudden breeze blows, and disperses the mist;
What had been hid therein now's uncovered:
And he sees... that the maiden he'd striven to kiss
Is... the girl... is... his abandoned lover!

'So then, this is how you vows and promises keep?
Remember my words? Now your role
In this life is to moan and incessantly weep,
And then — woe to your foul, faithless soul!

'In the silver lake's waves you no longer shall play,
Not for you now, with naiad to revel!
For your flesh will be swallowed by the voracious clay,
And your bright eyes snuffed out beneath gravel.

'By this tree here shall wake your perfidious soul!
For a thousand years let it remain —
In torment stretched out on Hell's e'er-blazing coals
With nothing to soothe the fierce pain.'

As he hears these words, he would escape from the lake,
Here and there he darts panicking eyes;
Then the wind of a sudden roars through the thick brake,
And the waters in foaming swells rise.

How the lake billows swell! How they roar and they hiss!
As the waters in maelstroms whirl —
Wide the gullet spreads of the aquatic abyss:
See him swallowed, along with the girl.

The water still rages, the billows still foam,
And still, in the dark moonlit glade
Two dim, errant shadows may be seen to roam,
Of a young man, it seems, and a maid.

She dances about the moonlit, silver flood,
He, at the larch, moans in deepest woe.
Who's he? He was keeper in the nearby wood;
Who's she? Well, I really don't know...

THE LITTLE FISH
(FROM A FOLK SONG)

From the village, the manor, a child
    Heartbroken, comes running near;
Her hair's undone, fluttering wild,
    And her cheeks are stained with tears.

At the edge of the meadow she stands,
    Where lake is fed by river,
And trembles there, wringing her white hands,
    Sobbing, with lips a-quiver:

'O my sisters, Świteź maidens, dear,
    Who in the lake waters swirl,
Swim close now, my darlings! And give ear
    To the plaint of a scorned girl!

'For I loved him, with all of my life!
    And to marry me he swore,
But he takes now a princess to wife —
    Poor Krysia he loves no more!

'Well, I wish them both a blessed life!
    May that hypocrite be gay
In the arms of his noble-born wife;
    But the girl that he betrayed

'Let them not mock! What now remains me,
    Abandoned lover, defiled?
Sisters, I come — what now restrains me?
    But... oh my child! Oh, my child!'

She says no more, no — but how she weeps!
    Then she closes her eyes tight,
Steps close to the brink, and then she leaps!
    The stream bears her out of sight.

Then through the woods from the manor's side
    Where bright lanterns gaily throng,
Laughing, the joyful wedding guests ride
    To feasting, dancing, and song.

Yet, mid carousing and revelries
    A child's cry pierces the night.
A servant emerges from the trees
    Cradling the wailing babe tight.

Toward the water he turns his steps
    Where willows, thickly twining,
Along the river as it slips
    The snaking banks are binding.

At last in a dark nook they rest.
    Sobbing, the lad cries, 'Alas!
Who will suckle this child at her breast?
    Where are you, Krysia, poor lass?'

'I'm here — beneath the rushing river,'
    Answers a voice, like soft sighs,
'The icy current makes me shiver,
    The gravel pummels my eyes.

'Over the rough-pebbled river-bed
    The currents batter me blue;
On coral and fly-larva I'm fed,
    My drink is the frigid dew.'

But as at first, the servant, distressed,
    Sobbing, moans anew, 'Alas!
Who will suckle this child at her breast?
    Where are you, Krysia, poor lass?'

And just then a little plop is heard
    Amidst the crystalline deeps.

The waters are troubled, as if stirred,
    And above them — a fish leaps!

And like a stone flung from a boy's hand
    Over the water will skim,
So the little fish skips toward land
    Wetly kissing the water's brim.

With scales of gold her bosom's shining
    On pretty red fins she speeds.
Her face is like a thimble tiny,
    Her two eyes are small as beads.

And then — the bright scales part and unfold
    And… those are a woman's eyes!
Above her white brow sprout locks of gold,
    See her slender neck arise!

Rosy cheeks now blush upon her face,
    Her breasts are like apples, firm;
She's fish-scaled from fin to comely waist…
    Now through the dry reeds she squirms.

Then she takes the baby in her hands
    And she rocks him tenderly,
Singing 'Hush now, hush, my little man,
    Lullaby now, don't you weep!'

And when at last the baby's at rest,
    His cradle amidst the woods,
She gives her child one final caress
    And again her face she hoods

In shining fish-scale of gold and gills;
    She dives, and she disappears,
And nought but the ripples on the rill
    Betray that she had been here.

What of the servant? Why, every day,
    Morning and eve, to the brook
He brings the boy so the fish-girl may
    Cosset him, and give him suck.

But then one day, to the waiting lass
    He failed to deliver
Her little boy. The hour came — and passed —
    But they're not at the river!

What was the reason for their delay?
    Well, the young lord and his bride
Chanced, on that evening, to stray
    Along the riverside.

Catching sight of them, the babe he hushed,
    And then wriggled safe among
Thick forest bramble, and screening brush
    To wait there. They waited long,

But no one returned along that way.
    He stood up, and tensed his sight,
But saw nothing. For the dying day
    Now ceded place to the night.

He waited on till the first star's gleam
    Made him bold enough to dare
To creep with the infant toward the stream,
    And — Good Lord! What he saw there!

Yes, where the crystal waters had rolled
    Above the deep riverbed,
Lies a sandy ditch, barren, and cold,
    Dusty and bleak, arid, dead!

Bits of clothing were strewn alongside
    Where the shore had once been, there;

Yet neither groom, nor his princess bride
    Were to be seen anywhere!

And then — his heart thumped — and he stood stock-
    Still — there, where once rushed the stream,
Loomed, in the moonlight, a lump of rock —
    Like two bodies, fused, it seemed.

A long while the servant stood there, shocked,
    An hour, two, and never stirred,
Until, at last, he corralled his thought
    And mumbled out a few words:

'Krysia! Hey! Krysia!' he calls and calls,
    And 'Krysia...' the wood echoes;
He looks around — there's no one at all;
    The streamlet no longer flows.

A clammy sweat prinks on his forehead
    Which he wipes with his free hand.
He looks at the rock in the stream-bed
    And nods. *Now, I understand!*

He glances down at the little child
    Now entrusted to his care...
He laughs (his laugh is a little wild),
    And hastens back home, in prayer.

[1819–1821]

PAPA'S RETURN
(A BALLAD)

'Go now, children, hurry to the hill
   On which the pillar stands, and there,
Beneath the Virgin's image kneel
   And raise a fervent, pious prayer!

'Papa's gone too long! Morning and eve
   You see me waiting, drowned in tears;
Swollen the streams, woods full of thieves
   And wild beasts — O, how I fear!'

She'd barely ended — the children run
   Off to the lonely crossroads where
The pillar stands; each and every one
   Kneels down in solemn, heartfelt prayer.

They kiss the earth. Then: 'In the Name
   Of Father, Son, and Holy Ghost,'
In ardent voices they proclaim
   Their trust in God's help at the post

Reciting one whole rosary,
   Our Father, and Apostles' Creed,
All that they knew by memory
   And then, following their brother's lead

From a prayer-book: the whole Litany
   To Our Lady's Immaculate Heart:
'Have mercy on Papa! Mercy!'
   They cry, each one singing his part...

And then comes a familiar rattle:
   The wagon! 'Papa's on the way!'
They leap, and cry, they squeal and prattle,
   And run to greet him, frisky, gay.

The merchant, seeing them rush near,
    Dismounts, his face with tears aglow:
'My sweets! What are you doing here?
    Did you miss your old Papa so?

'Mama — she's well? And Auntie? All
    Is well at home? I've got a treat
For you: raisins!' And big and small
    Out-shout each other; each would greet

Their Papa first with news from home.
    'I'll go with them. As for yourselves,'
(He tells his men) 'Go on alone...'
    Alas! They can't... for bandits twelve

Surround them all! Bewhiskered, rough,
    Wild-eyed and filthy (togs and mugs),
Dirks poking from each ragged cuff,
    Sabres in hand, or ugly clubs...

To Papa's side the children wail
    Cringing in fright, they shiver, shy
Behind his back; his face drains pale;
    He lifts his trembling hands on high:

'Take all you wish! Except this life.
    Let us go free — 'tis all I bid;
Make not a widow of my wife
    Nor orphans of these helpless kids.'

It seems his pleas fall on deaf ears!
    'Your gold!' one barks, and leaps aboard
The wagon; this, with club raised, nears
    The huddled group; that one, with sword

Threatens the carter. Then: 'Men! Cease!'
    A voice booms — the band's chief springs near —

'Go now,' he says. 'You are released.
    Be on your way, and do not fear.'

'Thank you!' sighs Papa. 'Spare your breath!'
    The bandit glares with angry eye.
'Long since you would have tasted death
    If not for... Let me tell you why.

'It's these your children you should thank
    That thus your life I deign to spare.
For, lurking here beneath this bank,
    I heard them raise their humble prayer.

'I knew that you would pass this way,
    A merchant, laden with rich goods,
And so I set a trap today
    To kill and plunder — So I should,

'If not for their incessant prayers.
    At first I laughed in spirit, jeered...
But then, some feelings, unawares
    Crept through my soul. I shrank with fear...

'For I recalled my distant home
    And sensed mercy begin to sway
My heart — I've a wife of my own,
    And son — who's no older than they.

'So, merchant! Be off to your city.
    I, to the woods, stained with my crimes;
Children, I beg you — of your pity,
    Recall me in your prayers sometimes.'

[February 1821]

MARYLA'S MOUND
A ROMANCE
An Idea from a Lithuanian Song

STRANGER, GIRL, JAŚ, MOTHER, GIRLFRIEND

    STRANGER
There, where the meadow green
Is split by Niemen's stream,
What is that pretty mound?
As if with chaplets ringed around,
With may-tree, thorn, and berry;
Its slopes with flowers merry,
Upon its summit grows
A copse thick with black cherry,
And from it spreads three roads?
One road leads to the right,
The second road: to that hut.
And I see the third one cut
Left. Tell me girl, if you might?
What is that pretty mound?

    GIRL
Ask the whole village round
And everyone's sure to give
The same answer. Maryla lived
In that hut; now, in that mound
She rests. The path to the right
Was worn by a shepherd's tread.
Along this other wends
Her mother; that, her girlfriend's
Road is — look! Now bright
Dawn breaks; quick — hide your head
Behind this pile of rubble —
They'll soon be here, and from this cover
You'll hear them vent their troubles.
Look right — here comes her lover,

And left, her girlfriend draws nigh,
And that woman — is her mother.
All tread slowly
All bring
Herbs lowly
In offering —
All cry.

    JAŚ
    O, Maryla — by this time
    I should have seen your face;
    We two should have embraced.
    See the young sun climb!
    Your lover awaits you!
    You lie abed, how long, how late! You
    Are angry with me, I fear!
    Ah, Maryla, my darling, my dear!
    Where is it you hide?
    No, you're not oversleeping,
    It's not anger that's keeping
    You far from my side,
    But the grave — for you have died!
    In this mound you lie covered,
    No more shall your lover
    Behold you, nor you him!
Before when I would lie me down to sleep
The hour of repose was sweet,
For shortly dawn would come again,
The two of us again would meet.
    Ah, then I slumbered deep!
But now I'll sleep here, severed
From all men; when I close my eyes, I may
See you in dreams again —
    Or perhaps I'll close my eyes forever!
I was a thrifty worker, diligent;
In better days
I won the praise
Of my neighbours and my father grey.

Now, hear my father lament!
But I, well, I've nothing to say
To man or God.
Blight take the seed! Rust scald the leaves!
Let all the unmilled grain must and rot;
Let the neighbours filch my sheaves!
No longer shall I drive
Wolf from the sheep-fold; what for?
    Maryla is no more!
My father promises me stock and store
Of brick and field, if I just take a wife;
Matchmakers come, angry, I drive
Them from my door —
    Maryla is no more!
Matchmakers, cease! I won't be wooing;
Father, I can't. Yes, I know what I'm doing!
I'm going on a long journey.
No more you'll see me — I'll not be returning
Ever. I'm off to Moscow to make war
On Russia — if they slay me, it will be
A favour. Life means nothing now to me
    Since Maryla is no more!

    MOTHER
I've overslept. What's the matter?
When all the folk are long haymaking?
You're gone, my dear, you're gone, my daughter —
Maryla! Who can ever waken
Me now? I sobbed the whole night long
And fell asleep only at dawn.
    My Szymon's out scything the grain
Since early morn on empty-stomach leaving
    Me sleeping, pitying my pain.
Go, cut your stalks and bind your sheaving,
For here I lie in the cold tomb.
Why should I go home now? For what?
Who sets my place in the dining room?
Who sits at table there, now I am not?

As long as you were with us, dear,
The house was one heavenly whirl.
All of your friends would gather here
To play, to laugh, each boy and girl;
Where was a brighter Lammas Day?
Where was Spring Sowing Dance more gay?
But now, my daughter, now you're gone!
Our home is like a desert waste.
Whoever draws near, passes on;
Door-hinges unrevolving, rust in place;
With moss our flagstone pathway's overgrown.
Both man and God now shun our vacant home,
    Maryla, Daughter! Now you're gone!

    GIRLFRIEND
    At dawn we used to meet
Right here at the waters;
I'd tell you about my sweet
And you'd tell me of yours.
    No more we'll chat of anyone
    Maryla, now you're gone!
To whom shall I reveal
What I most deeply feel?
    My thoughts, longings, and fears?
      Now you're no longer here —
My sadnesses — remain;
    My joy — is soiled with pain.

    STRANGER
All this he chanced to hear
    The stranger, and heartsick,
Wiping away a tear
    Left, with his walking stick.

[November 1820]

TO MY FRIENDS

ENCLOSING WITH IT THE BALLAD 'THIS I LIKE'

Kowno, 27 December

The clock strikes once, twice, thrice... and midnight tolls,
   A dead silence reigns all around;
I hear nought but the wind thumping these cloister walls
   And the barking of some watchful hound.

My candle is guttering low in its sconce
   And the brand in the grate sinks to ash;
So tallow and ember expire. Then at once
   A quick draught breathes, and once more they flash.

Frightful! Yes, but not so were those bright moments, fleet,
   When the heavens would tease us and blandish;
How many such moments! Ah, memories, sweet —
   Ha! What's the use to recall what has vanished?

And now, hunting happiness, through books I wander
   Just to grow bored, and shove them away;
Once again things delightful — and long-gone — I ponder...
   I start awake — dream again — stray...

At times, into such sweet delusions I fall
   That my lover, or brothers, I see —
And I leap up! — But — that shadow there on the wall
   Is cast... by no one other than me.

Better then to take pen in hand in the still night
   And to scrawl out some verse for a friend.
Whipping in my stray thoughts, I corral them, to write,
   I begin... but who knows to what end?

Should I write of my memories of the past spring
   To beat back the sharp midwinter chill? Ah!

A ghost-story, rather — with passion — I'll sing —
   Of ghouls, phantoms... and of my Maryla.

He who with camel-hair brush and oil would slay time,
   Let him paint her, and out-sublime art;
But the bard? Let him capture in immortal rhyme
   Her intelligence, virtue, and heart.

As for me — although all that is fresh to my mind
   It is solace I seek here, not fame;
And so if I am able, I'll tell you this time
   Of my late springtime, heartbroken game.

Maryla found terms of endearment... a chore.
   She dispensed them in tittle and drip.
She'd hear *I love you!* hundreds of times, or more,
   But *I like you* she'd never let slip...

To say nothing of *love*! So once, 'neath the moonlight,
   When all others were safely abed,
When it came time to bid my Maryla good night,
   I left her this ghost-ballad instead.

THIS I LIKE
A BALLAD

Look there, Maryla: where the woodlet ends,
   There on the right — a thickset willow ridge,
And on the left, a pleasant streamlet wends
   Through pretty meads, to slip beneath a bridge.

A steepled church, where nest owl and night-hawk;
   Beside it moulder piles of logs and staves.
Beyond the steeple, a bramble-patch, chock-
   Full of berry-bushes, and old graves.

A haunt of demon, or of cursèd soul?
   No one remembers. But in the deep night
No one among us, be he young or old
   Will pass the place without a flinch of fright.

As soon as midnight draws its gloomy pall
   Above, the church doors open with a crash;
In empty belfry bells begin to toll
   And something thumps and hisses through that patch

Where sometimes a pale light is seen to glow.
   Bolt after thunderbolt flashes and booms;
Grave-lids are pressed up, slid off from below,
   And ghosts are seen to spill out of the tombs.

A headless corpse now down the pathway strolls;
   And there a severed head speedily hies,
Champing its jaws as through the dust it rolls
   With flaming sockets where had once been eyes.

A wolf comes trotting near with padded stealth;
   You look — and he... broad eagle wings he's flapping?
Shout: 'Get thee behind me!' and you bless yourself —
   See? Off the wolf speeds, barking, howling, yapping.

Each traveller would fain avoid this road;
　None travel here but leaves behind a curse
For broken wagon-tongues, overturned load,
　Sprained oxen-legs and spooked or hobbled horse.

I, on the other hand, though old Andrzej tells
　Each of the danger, warning all away,
Would laugh at demons — who believes in spells? —
　And ride often here at midnight, whistling, gay.

Once though, at night, heading to your village,
　Our horses snuffled suddenly, and stopped.
They wouldn't set a hoof upon the bridge;
　In vain we plied both sugar-cube and crop.

The carter snapped the reins with all his might,
　Then — just as I'd dismounted — off they sped,
Leaving me stranded, lonely, in the night.
　I shrugged and smirked 'Well, this I like!' I said.

I'd barely finished, when from deep below
　The ghost of some girl, who perhaps had drowned
In the stream rose before me, robed white as snow,
　Her pale, moist brow with flaming chaplet crowned.

I couldn't run! I stood stock-still, amazed,
　My hair upstanding stiff upon my head,
Stuttering 'Let Christ's Name be forever praised!'
　And in reply 'For ever and ever,' she said.

'Whoever you may be, good honest soul,
　Who me, from purging torments have released,
I pray you happiness! May you grow old
　In good fortune, abundance, and in peace.

'You see before you a repentant soul,
　Who soon shall bask in everlasting bliss,

Whom you've now sprung from her purgative dole
   With those three words you uttered — *I like this.*

'The while the stars yet shine, before the crow
   Of the first rooster, I will here relate
My story — which the faithful ought to know
   So they might take a lesson from my fate.

'In those days, when my living lungs respired
   This atmosphere, Maryla was my name;
My father was the first man of the shire:
   Wealthy, and honest, of unspotted fame.

'His greatest longing was to see me married.
   That I was young and well-endowed, a scurry
Of lovers hastened — yes, no suitor tarried
   To vie for my charms — and my dowery.

'So many men to stroke my vanity!
   In their vain blandishments I so delighted,
The lower they bowed, my inanity
   Swelled the greater, as I scorned them all, and slighted.

'Józio came too — a youth of twenty springs,
   A fine lad he, both virtuous and shy;
Foreign to him were all sweet flatterings,
   Although the light of love glowed in his eye.

'I watched him wither. It was all in vain —
   Futile his tears and groanings, night and day;
A wild joy filled me as I saw his pain:
   He pales, despairs, while I laugh! Carefree! Gay!

'"I'm off!" he said through tears. "And none too soon!"
   I said. He died — heartbroken and alone.
Here, by this streamlet — see? — that mossy tomb
   Covers my lover's withered flesh and bones.

'Thereafter my days were empty, overlong.
   Too late a hardened heart like mine repents.
There was no way for me to right the wrong,
   And short the time remained for penitence.

'Then, once, while we sat late into the night
   A fearful, whistling whirlwind suddenly came —
And Józio's soul appeared to us — a fright!
   Like to a spirit doomed to Hell, aflame!

'Choking with sulphur, swept up off my feet,
   And whirled away from my parents through the smoke,
In which I heard wails and gnashing of teeth,
   And then, some voice, as it my verdict spoke:

'"You well knew, girl, that it so pleased the Lord
   To cull the female race from Adam's side,
Not to make his life aught to be abhorred,
   To punish him, but rather to delight.

'"But you, with heart of stone within your beast,
   As if to moaning deaf and unaware,
Never to be with love's avowals impressed,
   Unmoved by tear and groaning, plea and prayer,

'"For such severity, now, for long years,
   You'll writhe in Purgatory's sore abyss,
Until that time some living wight appears
   And sighs in your hearing, *Ah, I like this!*

'"Such simple words would have brought such delight
   To Józio — laughed to scorn, though bathed in tears;
You — beg in turn now! Not by tears, by fright
   Pleading your wretched alms, begetting fears!"

'He spoke, and soon I found myself in chains.
   One hundred years in torment I've been kept;

But when night falls, I'm freed from those great pains
    And I emerge from out the flaming depths.

'Then, in the church, or here, at Józio's tomb,
    Disdained by earth, unworthy of the heights
Of heaven, here I bore my heavy doom —
    To beg mercy in vain, haunting the nights.

'Fated to plead in terms that terrorise,
    Upsetting horse and cart along this pike,
All whom I halt but curse, anathemise —
    You are the first to chuckle, *This I like*.

'I'm grateful! And now this is granted me,
    To part the clouds, show you your future road.
You shall know a Maryla, too, but she...'
    At this — alas! — The dawn's first rooster crowed.

She bowed her face, now radiant and bright;
    I watched as she like gossamer film grew,
And then dissolved, just like a vapour, light,
    Through which a whispered puff of zephyr blew.

I gazed, and as the dawning sun now rolled
    Above — my horses safe beneath those trees —
I raised aloft, for all the suffering souls
    In Purgatory, three Hail Marys.

[1819]

THE GLOVE
(FROM SCHILLER)

    Aficionados all of bloody sport,
The King, along with all his court
Take their seats
In the arena where they bait the beasts.
And farther off, an awning covers
The knights who sit next to their lovers.

    The King nods. Let the games begin!
A grate lifts — and a lion comes padding in.
Slowly he strolls
And, lifting high his fearsome face,
Silently his eyes he rolls
And looks about the place.
He shivers, and his mane he shakes;
He roars, and all the region quakes,
Then slowly lets his fearsome body down
And stretches out upon the ground.

    The King frowns, and grunts:
See another grate rise,
And with quick pounces, eager for the hunt
Out a tiger flies!
He opens his mouth:
His fangs are flashing.
With tongue hanging down
And tail thrashing,
He circles the tawny lord of the pride,
With gaze reptilian
Roars — then grows still again…
To stretch himself out at the lion's side.

    Fashed, the King nods again:
A grate rises in answer

And from a single pen
Rush out two panthers!
The fierce cats, hungry for the fight,
Upon the tiger now alight.
The tiger opens wide his maw;
The tiger thwacks each with his paw.
But then the lion roars —
The battle's run its course:
The bloodied animals retreat
To lie down meekly at his feet.

   Then from the arcades there comes fluttering down
From beautiful Marta's hands
A glove, that lands
Smack in the centre of the baiting-ground
Where lion, tiger, panther, all recline upon the sands.

   Then Marta turns to Emrod, who loves
The lady: 'Sir, the time is now
To prove the heft of oft-repeated vow:
It seems I've lost my glove.'

   Without a moment's wavering, Emrod leaps
Over the rails and comes among the beasts.
Into their midst he boldly strides!
Awe strikes the ladies and the knights
To see him lift the glove, calmly retreat,
Re-leap the barrier and reclaim his seat.

   His lover greets him with joyous embrace,
And Emrod... flings the glove into her face:
'My vow fulfilled, I leave you now, Madame.'
And off he goes, thinking *Such love be damned!*

MRS TWARDOWSKA
(A BALLAD)

They eat, they drink, they dance and spin,
   They smoke, they tussle and they roll,
All but demolishing the inn:
   Hurrah! Ha, ha! Be gay, my soul!

Twardowski, arms akimbo, rests
   Like pasha at the table's end.
'Play on, my soul, play on!' he jests,
   On jokes and tricks his mind intent.

That bully soldier, drawing near?
   You see him pushing, shoving there?
Twardowski sweeps about his ear
   His sword — the soldier's now a hare.

That patron of the court, who laps
   In silence clean the frying pan?
Twardowski gives his purse two taps:
   A mutt is crouched where sat a man.

Then turns he to a shoemaker
   And drills a hole into his nose,
Before him setting a beaker,
   Into which pure Gdańsk vodka flows,

Of which he has a taste, as well,
   And then... into the mug he peers...
'There's something squeaking... What the hell?
   Hello — what are you doing here?'

There in the cup he found a sprite,
   A Teufelchen, a proper Kraut:
Short, fashionably clad, polite,
   He doffs his hat and then leaps out,

Lands on the floor and there he grows
   Two ells tall; with a cloven foot,
A long, unshapely, crooked nose,
   And hands like rooster claws to boot.

'Twardowski! Ah, my ancient crony!'
   He cries, and stamps his foot. 'Oh, please!
You mean to say that you don't know me?
   I'm your friend Mephistophiles!

'On Bald Mountain, you may recall,
   You deeded your immortal soul.
I've got it here — in your own scrawl,
   On ox-hide, writ in blood, all told.

'That's a forced rhyme. But all the same,
   Two years past, you were to surrender
To me in Rome. You never came…
   But here you are! It's time to render

'The devil's due… You look surprised.
   Ah, even tardy doves wing home
To roost, at last. Turn there your eyes —
   You see? This tavern's name is *Rome*.'

Twardowski leapt to his feet then
   At such a *dictum*, well, *acerbum*;
Mephisto caught him by the hem:
   'Fie! What of your *nobile verbum*?'

Well, what's to do? You can't trick fate;
   There's nought to do now but accept…
But then Twardowski's clever pate
   Brewed up a new shifty concept:

'All right, Mephisto, chum, you win.
   I soon must render up my soul.

And yet, before our trip begins
   Let's have one more look at that scroll...

'It says right here, in binding form:
   Before, from flesh, soul you out-fish,
Three services you must perform,
   Three last things — yes, whatever I wish.

'Three times yet I may harness you
   To labour for me, large or little,
Whatever I command — you do,
   Out-leaving neither jot nor tittle.

'Look there — upon the wall is tacked
   The image of a rearing steed.
Bring him here — saddle on his back,
   And make sure he's no plodding breed,

'But fiery. Then, if you are able,
   Twine me a riding crop of sand.
And don't forget — he'll need a stable
   To rest and munch on oats and bran.

'Of walnut-shell it must be reared,
   Its height Mount Krępak to exceed;
You'll thatch it with stiff Jewish beard
   And pave its floor with poppyseed.

'The thatch you'll measure with this nail,
   Inch thick each sheaf, and inches three
The length; as for the floor, impale
   On three brads every poppyseed.'

With spirit, Mephistophiles
   Sets to the task, and soon the horse
Is watered, fed, and combed; he weaves
   The crop of sand. And in due course

All is prepared. Twardowski leaps
   Upon the horse, he trots and canters,
Meanwhile the devil hammers heaps
   Of beard and seed. Twardowski banters:

'I am impressed, upon my soul!
   My second wish is a bit stricter:
Come, take a bath now in this bowl
   Brim-full of *aqua benedicta*.'

The devil gives a little yelp.
   He pales and shrinks and starts to sweat,
But the command given, there's no help
   For it — and so he seethes and frets

Up to his neck in woe. Then he
   Leaps out, sore, scalded, but he's won!
'The jig is up! And now, to me
   Your soul is forfeit. Let's go! Come!'

'Hold on! There's one wish left, you know:
   Before you pitch me into strife,
Permit me now, before we go,
   To introduce you to my wife.

'I'll take your place for one whole year
   In Hell, that bourne with torments rife,
If you can bear the same, right here,
   Living with her as man and wife.

'Vow her your lifelong love, respect,
   Faith, and boundless obedience.
But if you fall short in neglect,
   Our deal is done, we part as friends.'

The devil eyes the lass, with hair
   Horripilating on his nut,

Slinks to the door... He's almost there...
   He's made it! ...But the door's locked shut!

Twardowski's barred it! Round the room,
   Window to transom then he jets
Away, and up the flue he zooms...
   And some say that he's running yet.

TUKAJ or TESTS OF FRIENDSHIP
A BALLAD
IN FOUR PARTS

I
'I'm dying now. Why should I care?
And as for you — why, seize the day.
The grave will have us anyway —
And that's the end of all despair.
Far and wide the lands extend
Where I ruled: wealthy, famed; what's more
I never shut this castle's door
Before a stranger or a friend.
Alas! Humanity! And power!
Great palaces, great names are just
Great emptiness! Thin smoke and dust.
I'm young, and this — my final hour!
I hunted wisdom without rest,
Pursuing her through foreign lands.
On books I did much more than glance,
For learning's treasures I possessed.
But learning and wisdom are just
Great emptiness! Thin smoke and dust.
I kept the Lord's laws as I searched
His will, pure heart in trusting breast,
Awarding virtue with largesse,
Donating gladly to His Church,
To learn that trust and faith are just
Great emptiness! Thin smoke, and dust.
Creator! Why bestow such power
If, so young, I'm at my last breath?
Faithful retainers — What boots faith
To those facing their final hour?
You gave me a true lover. Why?
Since death poisons the wedding vow?
Friend, servant, wife, I leave you now
With empty hands. Be well! Good-bye!'

Thus Tukaj sinks abed, and faints
Amidst his friends' cries and laments,
Bidding the world farewell, he sighs,
And ebbing, weak, closes his eyes.

Then, lightning, with a fearsome boom
Pierces the roof; the castle walls
Shiver; then, in the midst of all
A stranger, pale, enters the room.
His grey hair flutters in the draught;
His wrinkled countenance is sere.
Below his knees tumbles his beard;
He leans upon a walking staff.
'Tukaj!' with rousing voice he calls,
And Tukaj leaps up at his roar.
They go — they're past the upper floor;
They pass through guards and castle walls.
And on they go, through the light rain,
Through the dark night, the swirling gloom.
Shivering free from the mists, the moon
Flashes, to be submerged again.
Through marsh and bracken Tukaj goes
With the old man. Kałdyczewo passed,
They skirt marshland and valley vast
Where Hnilica's strong current flows,
Past ready wastelands, speeding over
Steppes tawny, black, until they rest
Upon a granite rubbled crest —
The high summit of Mount Żanowa.
The old man kneels upon a grave,
Opens his mouth and winks an eye,
Then lifting both his hands on high
Shouts thrice, and thrice his staff he waves,
'Tukaj! Behold! You see that road?
That path winds through the marshy dell
To where the wise old man Polel
Who'd aid you, keeps his lone abode.
The wise would serve the wise. Come on!

Well-known, your learning and virtue;
Well-known, that God who fettered you
To mortal clay with loving bond
Granted you not overlong life —
But now, cast off all terrors vain,
Trust in Polel, be bold again,
And live for servant, friend, and wife!
Long years, whole ages, dare I say
Immortal life, first of all, I
Reveal now to your mortal eye.
So fate decrees, but such the ways
Of the inexorable fates
I may reveal it but to two.
If you trust someone through and through,
For sure — Eternity awaits!
Someone upon whom you depend
As your own self. Hit: immortal life.
But miss: torment, eternal strife,
Death, and punishment, without end!'
'Old man! Your words are deep,
Impenetrably draped, curtained,
I...' 'So, once more I shall repeat
Them: first you must select some friend;
Search through your heart, for on your choice
Of faithful friend or canny traitor
Your soul depends! A blessed state, or
An endless woe, bereft of joys!
Perhaps a trusted servant, then?'

   To this Tukaj makes no reply.
Who knows the hearts of other men?
And servants have been known to lie...
'Perhaps your lover, or your mate?
'Yes...' But he cuts short, looking askance,
'Yes...' he says, and hesitates,
Then, bites his lips, and wrings his hands,
'Yes, yes. My wife. Our wedding bands...'
And he believes, and yet he fears.

A blush upon his cheeks appears;
Ashamed, he wavers, wrings his hands.
He's thought it through. His answer is —
Nothing. Abashed, silent he stands.
'So, die! *You* dare to make demands?
You trust no one, it so appears —
Is it so bitter, then, to die?'
He thinks... 'I ask you once again:
A servant? Wife? Or any friend?'
By then a blackness floods the sky;
A rumbling makes the earth to quake.
Forests are burning, bogs are seething,
The cliffs and valleys all are breathing
Fire — flames dance upon the lake!
And then, amidst the flash and roar —
Was that God? Or some demon dread?
Once more Tukaj lies on his bed
Amidst his household, as before.
But — still an echo sifts like dust
Upon his ear: 'You have great wealth,
But no one you love as yourself,
No one at all, in whom you trust!'

II

  'I have a friend, I have!' Tukaj,
Near death, cries out — and look! For now
The pallor vanished from his brow,
A flash of health sparks in his eye!
The corpse is snatched from out the tomb;
The doctors gasp in wonderment.
He rises, walks about the room —
He rises! Under his own strength!
As if he never had been poorly.
And then — upon the pillow nigh:
A parchment sheet catches his eye,
Left by some crafty devil, surely,

Who'd written down the terms agreed.
This Tukaj takes in hand to read:

  'When the new moon has yet to show
Itself in the black heavens, go
Unto the mountain-grove — alone —
And there you'll find, beneath a stone,
A root of white. Tear it from thence;
When you're near death, command your friends
Your mortal frame to slice and quarter,
The root of white to boil in water,
And with the broth your flesh anoint —
Which then shall fuse whole, joint to joint.
And thus, body infused with soul,
You'll rise in youth's spring, fresh and whole.
So potent is this medicine:
You'll die, and rise, again and again.'

  There Tukaj sat, and as he read
He learned how to chop legs and head,
The broth medicinal to prepare:
What sort of herbs to toss in there;
Then, in conclusion, this adscription,
Appended as one last condition:

  'Item: Should our trust be abused
By the party that's to be used
Your cold limbs to anoint, anneal;
Should he the magic juice reveal
To other parties, the broth's might
Will vanish, and eternal night
Will be your lot; you'll not get well
But, dead still, tumble into Hell.
Now, if you dare accept this pact,
Sign on the dotted line here, please.
Our envoy, Mephistophiles
Will soon arrive to fetch it back.
You've been forewarned, you know our terms

Consider well: nobody squirms
Out of our pacts, or breaks our trust.
Given at Dan, in Erebus,
On Sabbath morning. Signing for
The Firm Infernal: Lucifer;
In witness to these binding pacts
I sign my name: Hadramelach.'

   This irked Tukaj, and gave him pause.
He'd been expecting no such clause!
Upon his fist he rests his chin,
And opening his tobacco tin,
Takes one pinch, two, of snuff; sidewise
He glances at the scroll with eyes
That droop now to the floor, in gloom;
He looks about his dining-room,
Picks up the scroll, sets it aside,
Reads through the contract once again,
Sets it apart, picks up a pen,
Puts it back down — he can't decide!
He makes a fist and with it, pounds
The desk-top, gnashes teeth, and sighs
And mops his brow; he makes to rise
Then sits again. But then he bounds
Up, waves his hand impatiently
And grumbles: 'Well then, let it be!'
Then, grows silent. Again he sits,
Again he'll think, again he'll rise,
To pace the room with angry strides;
If indecision gives you fits
Reader — patience! Forebear to cavil:
They're no trifles, pacts with the devil!

   So Tukaj ponders: Life eternal,
Or ever in the devil's grip.
He says nothing, musings internal
But tremble on his whispering lips.
Quick, quick! Decide! See how time flies!

And so, he leaves behind his friends;
The workshop of intelligence
Is where he must potter, alone.
And there the pact once more he seizes
— Eternal script of fell indenture! —
Both margins gripping fast, with pincer-
Like fingers, scanning while he squeezes
Sense from the infernal lines, he'll
Hesitate, and away he backs,
Till thoughts dripping like sealing wax
Spatter where he'd affix his seal.
Before he plunges, on the brink,
Such thoughts our Tukaj dares to think:
'The devil's in the details, great
Or petty; long I've been forewarned;
As for such small print, well, the form
Of all catches is triplicate:
To bring someone to commit treason
You need duress; sometimes, just reason;
Or gifts can work their hypnotism;
In short, we have this syllogism:
Greed, curiosity, and fear.
But he, whom these three cannot bend
To evil —threat, riddle, or wealth —
Such a one is the truest friend
In whom to trust, as one's own self!'

   Contented thus, into his hand
He takes pen, ink, and blotting sand
And moves to sign the sinful screed.
But, slowly, slowly, there's no need
For haste; the light's too dim, he thinks —
He fetches candles twain: the ink
Now, in the light, seems filmed with mould.
He grabs a new inkwell, the old
Spills out; sits at the desk again,
Picks up the pen — a sudden pain
Twinges his elbow. And — look there!

The nib is fouled with a thin hair.
When that's been dealt with, 'Hmm!' he grunts —
From too much scribbling, it's gone blunt;
He sharpens it; his lip he bites,
Then: LET IT BE is what he writes.
He wanted to subscribe his name
But ere he finished the cross-stroke
Of T a half hour passed and came
Around again, before he woke
Out of his musing; nothing more
He added but, ellipses.... four.

  He sat there gawking, as if smitten
At what upon the scroll he'd written —
You mock him, Reader? Come, be civil:
'Tis no small thing, pacts with the devil!

  But how he must have gaped in wonder
When he saw letter B distend,
And heard it fizz and buzz and thunder,
Swelling, filling from end to end
The parchment as warm moistened yeast
Makes swell the dough; before it ceased
Its spinning, roaring, and its thrumming,
The lower loop bulged like a tummy,
The upper now a pot-like head,
The down-stroke thin, like a wasp-waist;
A beak-like nose adorned the face
Above a goatish beard; instead
Of feet, he saw one cloven hoof
(The other was a rooster's claw);
An ox's eye, a furry paw —
In short, from all this warp and woof
Of beastly parts (not lacking fleas)
It was — why, Mephistophiles!

  Tukaj, with jaw dropped, at a loss:
Should he offer his guest a chair?

Or make a quick Sign of the Cross?
The devil boldly leapt from bare
Board, grabbed his little finger, then
He poked it with sharp vulture's beak,
And in the blood drop dipped the pen,
Thrust it in Tukaj's grip, though weak,
And slowly guided: U, K, A,
And when they'd finished with the J,
He snorted, whistled, then he vanished!
Where? Search him out, if you're so mannish.

[April 1820]

THE LILIES
A BALLAD
(FROM A FOLK SONG)

The strangest crime I've ever heard!
A woman kills her wedded lord?
Herself she buries whom she killed
Amidst the copse, beside the rill,
And on the grave mound, lilies plants.
(And as she tamps them down, she chants:)
'Grow my blossoms, reach as high
As he beneath you buried lies;
As he beneath you buried lies,
Grow my blossoms, thick and high!'

Now smeared in blood, behold her run,
The murderess-wife of man undone;
She runs through field, she runs through brush,
Through hill and dale, now up, now down,
The dusk is falling, breezes rush;
It's dark and gloomy all around.
She hears the cawing of a crow,
And owls hooting, deep and low.

On will she race, until she come
Where stands a birch tree, ancient, hoar,
Beside the hermit's humble home
And — *knock, knock* — knocks upon his door.

'Who's there?' The bolt slides, the old man
Opens the door, candle in hand,
And with a scream — to his surprise —
Past him the ghost-like woman flies.
'Ha, ha!' she cries, through livid lips;
As if possessed, she rolls her eyes,
White as a handkerchief, or slip:
'My husband! Ha! A corpse he lies!'

'Ah, God be with you, my dear girl —
What is it then that brings you here?
The night is deep, the stormwinds skirl;
Why traipse you through the forest drear?'

'Beyond the forest, past the spring,
The bright walls of my castle stand.
My man, with Bolesław the king
Made war in the Kievan land.
The months pass — year upon year runs —
No news of him! Alone I sleep...
The path of virtue is so steep!
And I — so young, among the young!
My troth to him I did not keep!
And now — O, my poor head! Alack!
I fear the King's assize! My man,
The husbands, they have all come back!

'Ha, ha! But he won't find me out!
You see this blood? You see this knife?
I stabbed! I stabbed! O, did it spout
The blood! I confess, I took his life!
Now, holy father, I beg you, tell:
What sort of prayers have I to say?
Where must I go to penance pay?
I'll crawl unto the gates of Hell!
I'll lash myself; for a long time
I'll wear sackcloth, just so my crime
Not merit eternal punishment!'

'O, woman!' says the old hermit,
'It's not in sorrow for blood spilt
That you come here? It's not regret,
But fear of censure for your guilt?
If so, be off now — go in peace.
Throw off your care, make bright your face;
Your secret's safe, and for all time.
Such is the nature of your crime:

What you have done, no others know
Save your husband. He's dead, and so
No one can call you to account
But he — and he's deep underground.'

He spoke, and she, greatly relieved,
Spun round, and was gone, as she'd come.
She ran straight home that very eve,
Uttering no word to anyone.
Her children met her at the gate.
'Mama,' they cried, 'it's getting late.
Where is our Father? Where's our Dad?'
'What?' she replied, 'where is the dead?
Your Dad, ha ha, is what I mean…'
(She didn't quite know what to say);
'He's in the woods, down by the stream.
He should be coming home today.'

The children wait. Two days pass. Three.
And still their father is delayed.
They wait a week, till memory
Of their father begins to fade.

Their mother, though, cannot forget,
Nor scour from out her mind her sin.
Guilt makes her heart sick with regret.
She never laughs; can't even grin,
Nor even closes an eye in sleep!
Night falls; just as she starts to drowse,
She hears a step scrape through the house,
As someone through the great hall creeps.
'Children, it's me!' she hears with dread
A raspy voice — 'It's me, your Dad!'

Long sleepless nights she spins abed,
Tossing and turning all the while;
Guilt makes her heart sick with regret.
She never laughs, nor ever smiles!

'Hanka,' she calls her maid, 'd'you hear
Those hoof beats on the bridge a-clatter?
Go out and see who's drawing near.
Shall we have guests? Or what's the matter?
Go out into the woods and see
If someone's coming to visit me.'

'Yes, Ma'am — they're heading here, I trust;
They race, kicking up clouds of dust,
On neighing stallions, glossy black,
The sun glints off their whetted swords
As they speed here along the track —
The brothers of your departed lord!'

'Greetings to our dear brother's wife!
How is your health? We trust you're well.
Where is our brother?' 'He's dead. He fell
Fighting for Bolesław. His life
Laid down for King and Country.' 'When?'
'O, long ago. Eight months... or ten,
He died, at war...' 'No! Those are lies!
Be of good cheer, and dry your eyes.
The war was over long before
That! Hale and hearty, soon you'll spy
Him, knocking at this very door!'

At this, her face drains ghostly white,
She faints, falls heavy to the floor.
Like one possessed, her eyes grow wide
And flit from window, wall, to door.
'Where is the corpse? Where is my man?'
Then, coming to herself again,
She flushes red, and would explain
Her faint as a sudden excess
Of joy, inquiring of her guests,
'When shall I then behold my dear?
When shall he stand before me here?'

'Why, he came back with us! Although
He spurred on faster; such his haste
To see you, his beloved, and throw
His arms around you; from your face
To brush your tears away. For sure
He'll be here soon. Perhaps today,
Tomorrow... He's wandering on the moor,
Poor fool; I bet he's lost his way,
In haste. A day or two more we'll stay
Until he comes. We'll send out men
To trace the paths and search the fen.
Tomorrow, you'll see him again.'

And so they waited. Sent out scouts;
A second day, a third... No track
Or trace, they never sniffed him out.
They weep, preparing to go back.

But she dissuades them. 'Brothers dear,
The Fall's unkind to travellers: rain...
Night falls so fast... the frost's severe...
Let me convince you to remain
Here till the Spring sun rises, warm.
You've waited so long; wait some more!'

And so they wait the Winter through,
But still nor hide nor hair of him.
Perhaps he'll come in March? In June?
They wonder, but their hopes grow dim,
For he is lying in his grave.
Above the mound the lilies wave;
Again they grow toward the sky,
As high as he below does lie.
The springtime comes, and fades away,
No more the brothers wish to stray...
Their brother's manor suits their taste;
Their brother's wife is young, and gay;
They must depart (they feign to haste),

Yet still they wait: another day,
Until the summer's last sun set —
And thus their brother they forget.

Their brother's manor suits them fine;
His young wife suits them just the same.
They both have been here the whole time,
So both smoulder in passion's flame.
The widow gives them both to hope,
And both are frightened at the thought:
To live without her? I can't cope!
Without her? Live on? I cannot!
As both in the same anguish toil
They go to her, to solve the broil.

'Listen, sister-in-law, dear:
Take our words for what they're worth.
Vainly do we tarry here.
Your man no longer walks the earth.
You still are young and fair of face:
To wither thus — what a disgrace!
Flee not the world. Choose you another:
In brother's place... accept a brother.'

They've said their piece. They stand and wait.
They burn with jealousy and ire.
One lets a word slip, low, irate;
The other's eye darts angry fire.
Their tight blue lips bite back harsh words,
But both are fingering their swords...

She scents the slowly-mounting fray,
But doesn't quite know what to say.
And so she asks them, *If they could,*
To wait a moment? And to the wood
She runs again, until she comes
To where the birch tree, ancient, hoar,

Stands near the hermit's humble home
And — *knock, knock* — queries him once more.

'How might I reconcile them friends?
I like them both, to tell the truth,
But both are bidding for my hand.
To whom the joy? To whom the ruth?
My small children are not yet grown —
I have great wealth to call my own,
And yet those lands will go to waste
Without good husbandry — disgrace!
But I'll have no more happiness;
No more shall I don bridal dress!
God's judgment looms above my head.
I'm plagued by nightmares in my bed;
No sooner do I lay me down
But the bolt's shot, and open creaks
My door; I hear the awful sound
Of breathing! It's him! Close he creeps,
My husband's corpse draws near my cot —
And in his hand — a knife he's got —
A bloody knife! And from his mouth
Sparks fly! He grabs me, pulls me out
Of bed — O, I've enough of fear
And terror — I cannot stay here!
Yet, where to go? Where might I rest?
I shall have no more happiness;
No more shall I don bridal dress!'

The hermit says, 'My daughter — hear:
No crime's without its punishment.
And yet, if you truly repent,
God will incline a clement ear.
I'm privy to God's mysteries...
Listen: I've got some news to cheer
You. Though your man's been dead a year,
Today, I still might make him rise.'

'What? What? How? O, good Father, no!
Not now! For that, passed is the time.
The fatal blade's between us, so,
We're cleft each from each by my crime!
I'm guilty — this I know four-square;
But any pains I'd gladly bear
If only I could lay the ghost!
I shall renounce all of my goods,
To a strict cloister I shall go!
I'll lose myself in the deep woods...
O Father, raise him? Never! No!
Not now! For such, passed is the time.
The fatal blade's between us, so,
We're cleft each from each by my crime!'

At this, the old man deeply sighs,
— A flood of tears brims full his eyes —
He hides in cowl his countenance
And sorrowfully wrings his hands.
'Marry anew. No longer wait.
Fear not the ghost that haunts his wife.
Of adamant is wrought death's gate —
The dead no more return to life.
No charms can raise your man, no spell,
Unless you call him back yourself.'

'But which of the two must I choose?
Which one will win, and which one lose?'
'I'd leave that question to the Lord.
Tomorrow, with the morning dew,
Let each set out across the sward
To pick, and then to wind for you
A wreath of blooms, with secret signs
Weft in the wreaths, a sure design
To indicate the maker. Then,
Let each one enter the Lord's home
And place them on the altar stone.

The wreath for which you stretch your hand —
Its maker shall be your new man.'

Delighted with the words she hears,
The widow longs to be a wife.
No longer ghost nor sprite she fears,
Never will he come back to life!
For that rests fully in her power,
And she'll never call him to her side,
Not even in her darkest hour!
So homeward now she turns her stride
(She left as quickly as she'd come),
Her perturbations pacified,
And speaks no word to anyone.
She runs through copse, she runs through lea...
She pricks her ear attentively...
She stops, and then resumes her pace.
Shh! What's that? Is she being chased?
She runs — Shh! What is that she hears?
Is someone whispering in her ear?
The darkness covers sky and land...

'It's me! Your husband — me! Your man!'

Again she runs, again she waits...
She halts, and then quickens her pace.
Her hackles rise; she cannot brook
To cast a trembling, backward look:
Again she hears, as on she rushes,
Someone is moaning in the bushes!
It echoes clear on either hand:
'It's me! Your husband — me! Your man!'

But now Sunday at last draws near;
Her hour of joy is almost here.
No sooner has the sun uprose
Than both the brothers hasten close.
Amidst her maids, with soft, shy tread

Toward the altar she is led.
She takes the first wreath in her hands
And sweeps the church with joyous glance.
'This wreath is plaited with lilies:
Pray, tell me. Whose blossoms are these?
Who is my man? Who is my lover?'

At this runs up the elder brother
With leap and bound, clapping his hands.
'They're mine! A lovelock of ribbons
Is woven among the lilies white.
This is my sign — you're mine by right!
I've won! I've won! I've won!'

'You lie!' exclaims the younger one.
'Just come outside and you will see
Where I plucked lilies on the lea —
Amidst the grove, beside the rill,
Upon a grave that lies there still!
I'll show you grave and stream, come on!
I've won! I've won! I've won! I've won!'

The angry brothers trade mad words,
Denying each the other's right.
Out of their sheaths they slip their swords,
With blood a-boil, prepared to fight.
Each would outscream the other one:
'I've won! I've won! I've won! I've won!'

The church doors boom shut as a rough
Wind roars and all the candles snuffs.
A figure enters, dressed in white,
Familiar arms, familiar tread,
And all there present quake in fright!
The spectre's words are fraught with dread:
'The wreath and woman both are mine!
These lilies from my gravemound grew —
Priest, take your stole our hands to bind!

O, murderous wife — woe betide you!
It's me! Your husband — me! Your man!
And you, my evil brothers, both
Tore blooms from my grave with your hand,
And now you're at each other's throat!
I am your brother! I'm your man!
You all are mine! Come, take these blooms —
It's time I led you to your doom.'

At this, the church floor quakes and splits.
Buttress is pulled from rib; the vault
And walls fall into the abyss
That yawned along the sudden fault.
The church is gone. Now, only trees
Stand near — and a field of lilies,
Which reach as far into the sky
As they beneath them, buried lie.

[May 1820]

THE MINSTREL[37]

Who is that long-beard, like a pigeon grey?
   Two boys lead him by the hand
   As along the edge of our land
Ready for harvest, he slowly makes his way.

The old man strums his lyre and trills
   A song, while the children play
   Small pipes; Go — call them back this way
And have them rest there, by that little hill.

'Come back, old man, and rest you over there —
   We're celebrating the tillage;
   It's not far to the village,
And what God's given us, we'll gladly share.'

He stopped, made a low bow, and back he walked;
   On either side of him the boys
   Crouched, near the hill, along the balk
Where they watched all the peasants at their joys.

The drums are thumping, and the pipers skirl,
   And round about the bonfire's blaze
   The oldsters drink, the maidens whirl
In celebration of the harvest days.

The pipes go silent then, as do the drums.
   Bonfire and dance are left behind
   And all the villagers now come
To where the ancient troubadour reclines.

'Greetings, old minstrel, in the Lord God's name!
   After your trek you must be tired —

---

37   An idea from a folk song.

Come and enjoy our harvest games,
And rest, and warm yourself before the fire.'

They lead him near a sumptuous table spread;
   They set him in the midmost seat
   And place before him vittles, bread.
'Perhaps you'll take a little cup of mead?'

'You've got a lyre, you've got two little flutes;
   Play us a little tune for three!
   We'll fill your bag chock-full of loot
In gratitude, glad for the melody.'

'Well, hush then,' he says to the gathered throng;
   He claps — and the murmurs all cease.
   If you wish, I'll play you a song.
What sort would you have?' 'Whatever you please.'

In his two hands he lifts mead-cup and lyre.
   He drinks deep and tunes the strings.
   His old bosom with the mead afire,
He nods to his pipers, they rise, he sings:

'From village to village I wander, I glide,
   As far as the Niemen is long;
   From forest to forest, beside
The River Niemen, I lift up my song.

'And all the villagers rush up to hear
   My songs — which they can't comprehend.
   Stifling my moans, drying my tears,
Once more my sad and lonely way I wend.

'If any should my sorrow understand,
   She would be pierced unto the core.
   We both would weep and clasp our hands,
And from there I should travel on no more.'

He pauses then; before once more he plays
   About the fields he casts a glance,
     And... something grips him... See him gaze...
Who is that — there — off to the side that stands?

She is a shepherdess — a wreath she's plaiting
   And unplaiting — bright, blooming strands.
     Next to her stands a youth, waiting
To take the woven chaplet from her hands.

An inner peace shines from her forehead bright;
   Her eyes are trained upon the ground.
     It's neither sadness nor delight
That grips her; rather, some notion profound.

Just as the dewy grass trembles at rest
   Though it be by no zephyr stirred,
     The linen rocks upon her breast
Although no breath or sigh of hers is heard.

Upon her bosom falls a yellow leaf,
   A little leaf from tree unknown;
     She looks and in soft — anger? grief?
Whispers it something — and now, look! She's thrown

It down; she turns away, moves off from there
   And heavenward she lifts her eyes
     That glitter with a sudden tear,
While on her cheeks some rosy blushes rise.

The minstrel's silent, strumming absently.
   Upon the shepherdess he pores
     With falcon's eye, and seems to see
What's hidden in her very deepest core.

He drinks a deep draught, he picks up his lyre,
   His pipers blow, he tunes his strings.

Once more his bosom glows with fire.
He strums the first chord, and again he sings:

'For whom, the wedding chaplet that you weave
   Of roses red, lilies and thyme?
   Happy the young man, I believe,
Who can say of your wedding wreath: Tis mine.

'For one lover alone thou'd wind
A wreath of lily, thyme, and rose.
Another lover would thee bind
But — not for him the wreath you wind.
Enough, the tears that make thee blind,
Spilt for another lover's woes,
When to another thou shalt bind
Thy fate with lily, thyme, and rose.'[38]

A murmur rumbles then, a rumour darts
   Among the crowd — a pallor falls.
   That song was heard around these parts
Before — but when? And who? No one recalls.

The minstrel lifts his hand, and stills the throng —
   'Give ear to me now, everyone!
   I'll tell you whence I have this song;
Who wrote it may have been a native son

'Of this village. Once, in my travelling,
   In Königsberg I found me;
   And there, a lad, crossing the stream
From Litwa met — a shepherd of this country.

'Oh, he was sad. But never did relate
   The history that made him groan;
   Later, abandoning his mates
He went away, never to go back home.

---

38   These triolets are taken from the poetry of Tomasz Zan.

'I often saw him wandering lonely
   In the dawn bright or moonlight hoar
     Over the meadows, out at sea,
Or on the sifting dunes of the sea-shore.

'Among the rocks, himself like to a stone,
   Wind or rain — it didn't matter,
     He'd give back to the wind his groans;
The tears he shed — back to the salty water.

'Once, I approached. He cast me a sad look,
   But never made to move away.
     I said nothing, but up I took
My lyre, and tuning it, did sadly play.

'His eyes grew teary, but he made a sign
   For me to play on, so I kept
     At it; he stretched his hand towards mine:
I took it, squeezed it, and both of us wept.

'We got to know each other; we grew fond
   Of one another; we became
     Friends. He, silent, as was his wont;
And I, on my part, kept still much the same.

'Then, when his frame with woe was whittled thin,
   And for himself he couldn't care,
     Servant and friend I stayed with him;
Yes, all throughout his illness I was there.

'I watched him as he slowly weakened, waned,
   And once he called me to his cot:
     "I sense soon I'll be past all pain,"
He said: "I'm resigned to the will of God.

'"My only sin was that my years unfurled
   In vain only to be tattered;

I've long been dead. If from this world
I must depart now, well, it hardly matters.'

'"When I to hide my face, to this wild sea
　These barren rocks, myself did bring,
　This world to me was as nothing
And I lived only in my memory.

'"How might I repay you?" squeezing my hand
　He said, "True to me, while I've lived?
　Repay such friendship? Nothing can.
But what I have, though meagre, I shall give.

'"I have this little twist of hair — pale, blonde,
　And dry sprig from a cypress tree;
　Take it, and memorise my song —
'Tis all the earthly treasure left to me.

'"Then go. Perhaps somewhere along the bank
　Of river Niemen, broad and deep,
　My love will greet your song with thanks;
Perhaps she'll see the sprig — and weep.

'"If she invites you near the cheery flame
　Of her hearth... tell —" but then, alas!
　He faded, with the Virgin's name
Upon his lips, but only the first half...

'He rallied once, but then, just as he died,
　Unable any more to speak,
　He pointed to his heart, and sighed
Toward the home his eyes did always seek.'

The minstrel paused, and with eyes sweeping round,
　Withdrew the sprig from out his breast;
　But there was nowhere to be found
Among the gathered crowd, the shepherdess.

Her face divine hidden in her kerchief,
   He only caught the sudden sheen
   Of her skirt flash; beyond his reach,
Led by some lad, never more to be seen.

The crowd rushed up, as he sat mesmerised:
   'Hey, old man!' they called, 'What's with you?'
   But he sat still, with far-off eyes,
And told them nothing — even if he knew.

Poems added to Ballads and Romances

(Leipzig, 1852)

THE LURKERS
(A UKRAINIAN BALLAD)

From the black garden's depths, rushes in, out of breath,
  The palatine, in fury and fear,
Running all through the house, in search of his young spouse…
  Reaches bedroom: 'There's nobody here!'

With black bile swells his liver; his hands — how they quiver!
  As he broods, sunken deep now in gloom.
Then he shakes his grey head, turns away from the bed,
  And he summons his Cossack Naum.

'Hey, you stupid old Cossack! How come there's not out back
  At night dog, guard — no one at all?
Get a move on, you lout! Get the gunpowder out
  And take my Turkish gun from the wall!'

With so deadly a burden, they into the garden
  Creep, where, bathed in the silver moonlight,
Seated on the soft swarth something glows in the dark:
  'Tis a young girl, in nightgown of white.

With one hand the young maid frets with one golden braid
  While the other her bosom doth cover;
Then in modest alarm, she shrugs off the stout arm
  Of a man kneeling near her — a lover!

But he, pressing her knees, urges, 'Darling! Sweet! Please!
  Can it be that I've lost everything?
Can it be that one buys a girl's pettings and sighs?
  Can gold chime with so thrilling a ring?

'Though he may buy and barter, he can't match my ardour —
  Our true passion — that nothing can sever!
He's just cunning and cold. He's got nothing but gold.
  And you've sold yourself to him, forever?

'Every night he shall rest on your downy-white breast,
    To my lamb pressing his goatish head!
Your red lips he shall crush, snuffling those cheeks ablush,
    On the honey forbidden me — fed!

'Now, each night on my horse, 'neath the moon here I'll course,
    Though the cold or the storm fiercely presses,
Just to greet you with sighs — Greetings? Painful goodbyes!
    Wishing you — tolerable caresses!'

Though no longer she'd hear, still he sifts in her ear
    More reproaches, or maybe fresh charms,
Till fainting, she relents, she gives up all defence
    And she folds herself into his arms.

This the lurking pair sees, hidden in the thick trees
    And they pull two lead rounds from their sack;
Each then powder-pack rips, ball and wadding then slips
    Down the barrel, with ramrod to pack.

Then the Cossack cries: 'Master! Devil take it! Disaster!
    I can't shoot that girl or that man —
As I readied the flint, something bit in my squint
    And a tear's fouled the charge in the pan!'

'So your powder's not dry? Lout! I'll teach you to cry!
    Here: this fresh powder on the pan spread;
Cock the hammer, take aim, don't you blubber again!
    Put that bullet in her — or your head!

'Higher aim... right, a jot... now, hold fire till I've shot.
    The young groom first shall perish. He's mine!'
But, not heeding his squire, the old Cossack did fire:
    Whom he brought down was — the Palatine.

THE ESCAPE
(A BALLAD)

A full twelve months, the one she's cherished
Is off warring. Has he perished?
Maiden! Your youthful years are wasting!
From the Prince matchmakers are hastening.

The Prince is feasting in his keep
While in her room the Maiden weeps.

Her eyes once flashed like lightning bolts.
Today, they gush muddy and cold.
Her face, once like the full-moon bold,
Wanes to the shadow of itself:
Her beauty's wasting, and her health.

Her mother wrings her careworn hands;
The priest has just proclaimed the banns.

Matchmakers press her, from the groom.
'They'll lead me to no altar, merry,
But broken, to the cemetery.
If he's dead, so am I! And you,
Mother, of mourning you'll die too!'

The priest waits with his purple stole.
Go, child, to the confessional.

Then comes this old hag, sharp and rare:
'Chase that relic-juggler away!
God and faith — dream and nightmare!
But I know how to make you gay.
Wise-women can make all things well,
With herb and charm and other shift.
Have you still any of his gifts?
Come now — I'll brew a mighty spell.

Twist his lovelock into an asp.
With it, two wedding bands now clasp.
We need some blood. Here, prick your hand,
Drip it on asp and wedding-bands,
Now — on the asp we breathe — that's right.
Our curse will have such force, such might
That he must come for you tonight!'

The Maiden sins — the rider spins
Quick on his way — sharp to obey
The curse — he's passed the threshold drear.
Maiden, Maiden, have you no fear?

The castle slumbers, all is quiet,
The Maiden watches — now midnight
Strikes; silent are the castle guards
But — Listen! — Hoofbeats strike the sward!
The mastiff howls, and shivers, listening;
Along his spine his fur is bristling!

The lower gates screech rustily;
Now heavy boots thump in the hall
And doors creak open: one, two, three,
Though they'd been locked fast, one and all!
The rider enters, all in white,
And takes a seat at her bedside.

Ah, sweet and swiftly flows the time!
An owl hoots, and at the gate
A horse neighs. 'Be well, lover mine,
Hear my steed neigh? It's getting late.
The dawn soon comes lovers to sever
Or... Come with me! Be mine forever!'

Beneath the moon, through mist and gloom,
The rider speeds o'er brambles sere:
Maiden, Maiden, have you no fear?

Like wind the horse flies through the meads.
The woods are silent — on he speeds;
The woods crouch stilly — nothing stirs;
Some startled crows caw in dead firs,
And from deep dens flash wolvish eyes
Like candles, glittering in surprise.

   'Giddap, my steed, my trusty mount,
   The hour is late, the time it flies.
   Before the moon sinks from the skies
   We've ten cliffs that we must surmount,
   Nine mountains steep, nine streams swift-flowing,
   Before the first rooster be crowing.'

'Where are you taking me now?' 'Why —
To Mount Mendog — there is my home.
Along that road all men may roam
By day; by night, we slip round, sly.'
'Have you a keep?' 'Deep in these rocks,
And secure — though it has no locks.'
'O lover mine, pull up your steed!
I'm frightened here in this strange land!'
'Grip tighter to my saddle, sweet...
What's that you have there in your hand?
Is that some knitting-box you took?'
'Ah no — this is my prayer book.'

'We can't slow down, we must make haste.
You hear those hoofbeats drum the sod?
Before us lies a chasm broad.
Throw away the book — we're being chased.'

   Disburdened of the weight, the charger
   Surges a full ten miles farther.

And now through marsh and bog they're fleeting,
Empty wastes. Wills-o'-the'-wisps
Flash just before them, as if leading

Them on — from tomb to tomb one slips
And as it skips it leaves a pale
Blue smudge behind it, like a trail.
The rider follows it, as it sails.

'O lover mine! Where does it lead
This road, where there's no trace of man?'
'Good path indeed, when there's a need
To flee as fast as flee one can.
There are no such highroads that run
To my estate, where no guests come,
Where no rich toff in four-in-hand
Is driven by his serving-man.

  'Giddap, my steed, giddap, brave beast!
  The dawn is blushing in the east.
  Before the matins-bell resounds
  We must be well past several mounds,
  A couple crests, and streams swift-flowing
  Before the second cock be crowing.'

'O lover mine, rein in the steed!
He's spooked, and so he's gone astray —
So many trees lie thwart the way
I'm knocked against them; scratched, I bleed!'
'My darling, what's that string I see
That dangles from your pocket there?'
'My lover, that's my rosary.
The other is my scapular.'

'O, the damned necklace! Cast it wide
Away! It blinds the charger's eyes!
See how he shivers, shunts aside —
Throw it away!' As off it flies,
Terror removed, see how the charger
Surges a full five miles farther.

'What do I see, love, in the gloom?
A graveyard!' 'That's my castle wall.'
'And those crosses? And those stone tombs?'
'They're not crosses, but bastions tall.
As soon as we've speeded therein
Our journey will be at an end.

'My trusty steed! Past cliff and river
You've brought us safely home again
Before cock-crow... I know, you shiver:
That cross gives both you and me pain.'

'O lover mine — where are we going?
Why have we stopped? I'm soaked with dew,
And now a chilly wind is blowing.
Lend me your coat — I'm frozen blue!'
'My darling girl! Here, let me rest
My head upon your trembling breast.
My brow's afire so, it alone
Might warm the thickest, coldest stone.

'But what's that spike you have, of steel?'
'A cross my mother gave me — gold...'
'Throw it away! So sharp, I feel
It pierces me unto the soul!
It tears my cheek, it burns my brow,
Toss far away that sharp spike — now!'

The cross fell to the earth. Soon after,
The rider threw his arms about
The maiden — fire burst from his mouth
And eye-sockets, and human laughter
Erupted from the horse, who flew
Over the walls as the cock crew
And the bells rang for morning Mass.
On his way there, the rector passed
The graveyard — nowhere to be found
Horse, rider, Maiden — all around

ADAM MICKIEWICZ

Was quiet, but in the lifting gloom
He saw — one fresh and crossless tomb.

    Long mused he, while the matins tolled,
    That day, he said Mass for two souls.

THE THREE BUDRYSES
(A LITHUANIAN BALLAD)

Budrys calls his three sons, stout Lithuanians,
   To the porch to deliver these words:
'Get your steeds one and all, saddle, girth and headstall,
   And your finely-honed spears and your swords.

'For all Wilno is shouting — there can be no doubting —
   They're drumming for three foreign fights:
Olgierd's hitting the Russians, Skiergiełł: their Polish cousins
   And Prince Kiejstut — the Teutonic Knights.

'Every healthy, big-boned man must now serve his homeland,
   In the gods of great Litwa be bold;
Though this year I shall not go, I'll see my sons off. So:
   There are three of you: each his own goal.

'One of you three must soldier in Russia with Olgierd
   At the Ilm, where Novogrod's the prize;
There is fur of the marten and silvery curtains,
   And coin plentiful as the ice.

'You, then: head with Kiejstut on the road to the Teuton
   Exterminate those German pests!
They've more amber than the sands, rich linen on all hands,
   Golden brocade in which their priest vests.

'You, the third with Skiergiełł then, you're bound past the Niemen,
   Where there aren't much riches to hide.
But with our Polish neighbours you'll find shields and sabres
   And something still better: a bride.

'For the Lach girls are lovers surpassing all others!
   They're feisty and playful as kittens;
They've cheeks whiter than milk, lashes soft as black silk,
   And their eyes flash like stars when they're smitten.

'Half a century's past since I swiped such a lass
   From the Poles, and I gave her my heart;
Though she's no longer here, still my eyes fill with tears
   When they chance to glance toward those parts.'

Finishing his account, he saw all his sons mount,
   And they thundered off, each with his aim;
Summer, fall, winter, spring — still they're not returning.
   Budrys reckons them dead, battle-slain.

Then, through blizzard and din, see: a knight's riding in!
   With something wrapped in cloaks at his side.
'What've you got there, my son? Roubles from the Russian?'
   'Father, no — 'tis my young Polish bride.'

Through the blizzard and din — someone else, riding in!
   With ought wrapped in furs, snug by his side:
'German amber, I think? Stuffed in that pelt of mink?'
   'No, dear father, 'tis my Polish bride.'

Through the blizzard and din comes a third riding in
   With some loot — a king's ransom, at least!
But before the lad shows, Budrys already knows —
   He must lay out a third wedding feast.

THE RENEGADE
(A TURKISH BALLAD)

What happened lately in Iran
   I'll tell the world entire.
To his cashmere harem divan
   A pasha once retired.

Maids Greek and maids Circassian sing
   With girls raped from the Khirgiz;
Blue eyes among the former wink,
   The latter's are black like Eblis.

The pasha neither sees nor hears,
   His eyes a turban shrouds.
He drowses, and puffs from hookah blear
   And aromatic clouds.

Then at the door the eunuchs twirl
   In graceful homage bending:
Kryzlar-Aga leads in a girl,
   Bows deeply, says: 'Effendy!

'Whose brightness is of such great might
   Amidst the starry divan,
As midst the diamonds of the night
   The blaze of Aldeboran!

'Deign flash here, Star of the Divan:
   The news I bring is sweet:
Your servant-breeze from Lechistan
   Wafts tribute to your feet.

'Not even the Padishah can
   Boast such a blossom white
As this bloom — from that frigid land
   You recall with such delight.'

The gauze veil that subdued her grace
    Was lifted — all there gasped;
The pasha glanced upon her face...
    The hookah, from his grasp

Fell, as he too, helpless now, and frail
    Collapsed upon his bed;
His lips went livid, his cheeks pale:
    The renegade — was dead!

BIBLIOGRAPHY

Primary Sources

MICKIEWICZ, Adam. *Dzieła poetyckie*, ed. Stanisław Pigoń. Warszawa: Czytelnik, 1983.

MICKIEWICZ, Adam. *Poezye, Tom pierwszy*, ed. Leonard Chodźko. Paris: Barbezat i Delarue, 1828.

MICKIEWICZ, Adam. *Ballady i Romanse*. Lipsk: Brockhaus, 1852.

Secondary Sources

BRÜCKNER, Aleksander. *Mitologia słowiańska i polska*. Warsaw: PWN, 1985.

BRZOZOWSKI, Jacek. 'Głosy do "Romantyczności"', *Prace Polonistyczne*, seria XLIX (1994), pp. 7-48.

CYSEWSKI, Kazimierz. 'Ballady i romanse — przewodnik epistemologiczny,' *Pamiętnik Literacki: czasopismo kwartalne poświęcone historii i krytyce literatury polskiej*, 74/3 (1983), pp. 65-100.

ERBEN, Karel Jaromír. *Kytice z básní*. Praha: Jaroslav Pospíšíl, 1861.

KOLLÁR, Ján. *Slávy dcera. Báseň lyricko-epická v pěti zpěvích*. Praha: Nákladem knihkupectví I.L. Kobera, 1868.

KRASZEWSKI, Charles S. 'Revenant Spirits in Slovak Folk Narrative Poems,' *Kosmas*, Vol. 20, No. 2 (2007), pp. 1-27.

KUZIAK, Michał. *Inny Mickiewicz*. Gdańsk: Słowo/Obraz terytoria, 2013.

LIBERA, Leszek. 'Mickiewicz als Übersetzer des Schillerschen "Handschuhs", *Zeitschrift für Slavische Philologie*, Vol. 47, No. 2 (1987), pp. 289-307.

LUKAS, Katarzyna. 'Der romantische Protagonist als Träger des katholischen Weltbildes. Über den IV. Teil des dramatischen Fragments *Dziady* von Adam Mickiewicz in deutschsprachigen Übersetzungen,' *Studia Germanica Posnaniensia*, XXX (2006), pp. 5-33.

MÁCHA, Karel Hynek. *Spisy, Díl první*. Praha: Nákladem knihkupectví I.L. Kober, 1862.

MICKIEWICZ, Adam. *Balady a romance*, tr. Josef Matouš, František Halas, Vladimír Holan. Praha: Vyšehrad, 1953.

MICKIEWICZ, Adam. 'O poezji romantycznej,' in Adam Mickiewicz, *Pisma*. Paris–Leipzig: E. Jung Treuttel-Franz Wagner, 1861.

MICKIEWICZ, Adam. *Forefathers' Eve*. London: Glagoslav, 2016.

SKVOR, Georges. 'Le romantisme polonaise et tchèque au XIXe siècle,' *Études Slaves et Est-Européennes / Slavic and East-European Studies*, Automne/Autumn 1956, Vol. 1, No. 3, pp. 164-178.

SZELWACH, Grzegorz. *Listy Adama Mickiewicza*. New York: PIASA Books, 2006.

ŠTÚR, Ľudovit. *Slavdom. A Selection of his Writings in Prose and Verse*. London: Glagoslav, 2021.

VONGREJ, Pavol. *Diamant v hrude. Sládkovičova* Marina. Martin: Matica slovenská, 1970.

WALC, Jan. *Architekt Arki*. Chotomów: Verba, 1991.

ABOUT THE AUTHOR

Adam Mickiewicz (1798–1855) is the national poet of Poland. He was successful in every genre that he took in hand, setting the benchmark for excellence in poetry, prose and drama, for all the writers that came after him. His lyric poems, collected in *Ballads and Romances* (1822), ushered in the Romantic Movement in Polish literature. His narrative poems, *Grażyna* (1823) and *Konrad Wallenrod* (1828), reveal his sustained mastery of longer poetic genres. Mickiewicz's epic in twelve books, *Pan Tadeusz* (1834), is universally recognised as Poland's national epic, as well as the last Virgilian epic composed in Europe. *Forefathers' Eve* (available in English translation from Glagoslav) is a four-part monumental drama that deals both with particular themes of Poland's subjugation to the empires of Russia, Prussia and Austria, and general themes — the sense of love, both erotic and Platonic, time and eternity, fellowship and the Communion of the Saints. Compared to the work of Dante and Goethe, it is this masterpiece of Polish monumental drama that elevates Mickiewicz to the ranks of what Eliot liked to call the 'great Europeans.' Among Mickiewicz's prose works, his lectures at the Collège de France on Slavic Literature are noteworthy. Adam Mickiewicz died in southern Europe while attempting to recruit troops to fight against the Tsarist empire.

ABOUT THE TRANSLATOR

Charles S. Kraszewski (b. 1962) is a poet and translator, creative in both English and Polish. He is the author of three volumes of original verse in English (*Diet of Nails*; *Beast*; *Chanameed*), and one in Polish (*Hallo, Sztokholm*). He also authored a satirical novel *Accomplices, You Ask?* (San Francisco: Montag, 2021). He translates from Polish, Czech and Slovak into English, and from English and Spanish into Polish. He is a member of the Union of Polish Writers Abroad (London) and of the Association of Polish Writers (SPP, Kraków). In 2022 he was awarded the Gloria Artis medal (III Class) by the Ministry of Culture of the Republic of Poland.

DRAMATIC WORKS
by Cyprian Kamil Norwid

'Perhaps some day I'll disappear forever,' muses the master-builder Psymmachus in Cyprian Kamil Norwid's *Cleopatra and Caesar*, 'Becoming one with my work…' Today, exactly two hundred years from the poet's birth, it is difficult not to hear Norwid speaking through the lips of his character. The greatest poet of the second phase of Polish Romanticism, Norwid, like Gerard Manley Hopkins in England, created a new poetic idiom so ahead of his time, that he virtually 'disappeared' from the artistic consciousness of his homeland until his triumphant rediscovery in the twentieth century.

Chiefly lauded for his lyric poetry, Norwid also created a corpus of dramatic works astonishing in their breadth, from the Shakespearean *Cleopatra and Caesar* cited above, through the mystical dramas *Wanda and Krakus, the Unknown Prince*...

Buy it > www.glagoslav.com

THE SONNETS
by Adam Mickiewicz

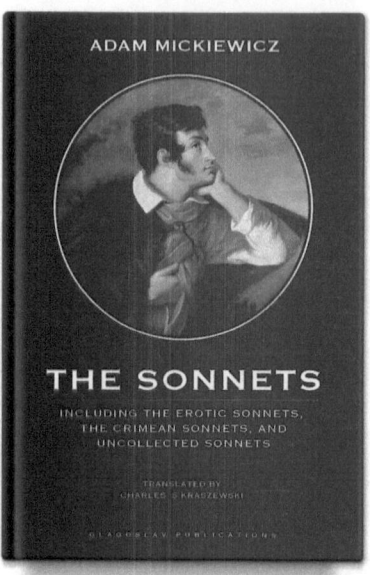

Because the poetry of Adam Mickiewicz is so closely identified with the history of the Polish nation, one often reads him as an institution, rather than a real person. In the *Crimean and Erotic Sonnets* of the national bard, we are presented with the fresh, real, and striking poetry of a living, breathing man of flesh and blood. Mickiewicz proved to be a master of Petrarchan form. His *Erotic Sonnets* chronicle the development of a love affair from its first stirrings to its disillusioning denouement, at times in a bitingly sardonic tone. *The Crimean Sonnets*, a verse account of his journeys through the beautiful Crimean Peninsula, constitute the most perfect cycle of descriptive sonnets since du Bellay. *The Sonnets* of Adam Mickiewicz are given in the original Polish, in facing-page format, with English verse translations by Charles S. Kraszewski. Along with the entirety of the Crimean and Erotic Sonnets, other "loose" sonnets by Mickiewicz are included, which provide the reader with the most comprehensive collection to date of Mickiewicz's sonneteering. Fronted with a critical introduction, *The Sonnets* of Adam Mickiewicz also contain generous textual notes by the poet and the translator.

Buy it > www.glagoslav.com

FOREFATHERS' EVE
by Adam Mickiewicz

Forefathers' Eve [*Dziady*] is a four-part dramatic work begun circa 1820 and completed in 1832 – with Part I published only after the poet's death, in 1860. The drama's title refers to *Dziady*, an ancient Slavic and Lithuanian feast commemorating the dead. This is the grand work of Polish literature, and it is one that elevates Mickiewicz to a position among the "great Europeans" such as Dante and Goethe.

With its Christian background of the Communion of the Saints, revenant spirits, and the interpenetration of the worlds of time and eternity, *Forefathers' Eve* speaks to men and women of all times and places. While it is a truly Polish work – Polish actors covet the role of Gustaw/Konrad in the same way that Anglophone actors covet that of Hamlet – it is one of the most universal works of literature written during the nineteenth century. It has been compared to Goethe's Faust – and rightfully so...

Buy it > www.glagoslav.com

A BURGLAR OF THE BETTER SORT
by Tytus Czyżewski

The history of Poland, since the eighteenth century, has been marked by an almost unending struggle for survival. From 1795 through 1945, she was partitioned four times by her stronger neighbours, most of whom were intent on suppressing if not eradicating Polish culture. It is not surprising, then, that much of the great literature written in modern Poland has been politically and patriotically engaged. Yet there is a second current as well, that of authors devoted above all to the craft of literary expression, creating 'art for art's sake,' and not as a didactic national service. Such a poet is Tytus Czyżewski, one of the chief, and most interesting, literary figures of the twentieth century. Growing to maturity in the benign Austrian partition of Poland, and creating most of his works in the twenty-year window of authentic Polish independence stretching between the two world wars, Czyżewski is an avant-garde poet, dramatist and painter who popularised the new approach to poetry established in France by Guillaume Apollinaire, and was to exert a marked influence on such multi-faceted artists as Tadeusz Kantor.

Buy it > www.glagoslav.com

THE MOUSEIAD AND OTHER MOCK EPICS
by Ignacy Krasicki

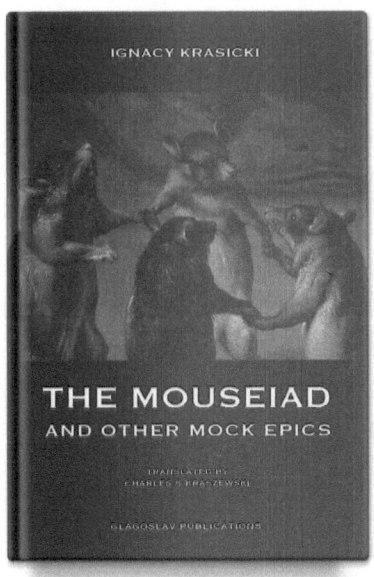

International brigades of mice and rats join forces to defend the rodents of Poland, threatened with extermination at the paws of cats favoured by the ancient ruler King Popiel, a sybaritic, cowardly ruler... The Hag of Discord incites a vicious rivalry between monastic orders, which only the good monks' common devotion to... fortified spirits... is able to allay... The present translation of the mock epics of Poland's greatest figure of the Enlightenment, Ignacy Krasicki, brings together the *Mouseiad*, the *Monachomachia*, and the *Anti-monachomachia* — a tongue-in-cheek 'retraction' of the former work by the author, criticised for so roundly (and effectively) satirising the faults of the Church, of which he himself was a prince. Krasicki towers over all forms of eighteenth-century literature in Poland like Voltaire, Swift, Pope, and LaFontaine all rolled into one. While his fables constitute his most well-known works of poetry, in the words of American comparatist Harold Segel, 'the good bishop's mock-epic poems [...] are the most impressive examples of his literary gifts.' This English translation by Charles S. Kraszewski is rounded off by one of Krasicki's lesser-known works, *The Chocim War*, the poet's only foray into the genre of the serious, Vergilian epic.

Buy it > www.glagoslav.com

OLANDA

by Rafał Wojasiński

I've been happy since the morning. Delighted, even. Everything seems so splendidly transient to me. That dust, from which thou art and unto which thou shalt return — it tempts me. And that's why I wander about these roads, these woods, among the nearby houses, from which waft the aromas of fried pork chops, chicken soup, fish, diapers, steamed potatoes for the pigs; I lose my eye-sight, and regain it again. I don't know what life is, Ola, but I'm holding on to it. Thus speaks the narrator of Rafał Wojasiński's novel *Olanda*. Awarded the prestigious Marek Nowakowski Prize for 2019, *Olanda* introduces us to a world we glimpse only through the window of our train, as we hurry from one important city to another: a provincial world of dilapidated farmhouses and sagging apartment blocks, overgrown cemeteries and village drunks; a world seemingly abandoned by God — and yet full of the basic human joy of life itself.

Buy it > www.glagoslav.com

GŁOSY / VOICES
by Jan Polkowski

In December 1970, amid a harsh winter and an even harsher economic situation, the ruling communist regime in Poland chose to drastically raise prices on basic foodstuffs. Just before the Christmas holidays, for example, the price of fish, a staple of the traditional Christmas Eve meal, rose nearly 20%. Frustrated citizens took to the streets to protest, demanding the repeal of the price-hikes. Things took an especially dramatic turn in the northern regions near the Baltic shore — later, the cradle of the Solidarity movement, which would eventually spark the fall of communism in Poland and throughout Central and Eastern Europe — where the government moved against their citizens with the Militia and the Army. Forty-one Poles were murdered by their own government when militiamen and soldiers opened fire with live rounds on the crowds in Gdańsk, Gdynia, Szczecin and Elbląg.

Jan Polkowski's moving poetic cycle *Głosy* [Voices], presented here in its entirety in the English translation of C.S. Kraszewski, is a poetic monument to the dead, their families, and all who were affected by the 'December Events,' as they are sometimes euphemistically referred to.

A BILINGUAL EDITION

Buy it > www.glagoslav.com

ABSOLUTE ZERO

by Artem Chekh

The book is a first person account of a soldier's journey, and is based on Artem Chekh's diary that he wrote while and after his service in the war in Donbas. One of the most important messages the book conveys is that war means pain. Chekh is not showing the reader any heroic combat, focusing instead on the quiet, mundane, and harsh soldier's life. Chekh masterfully selects the most poignant details of this kind of life.

Artem Chekh (1985) is a contemporary Ukrainian writer, author of more than ten books of fiction and essays. *Absolute Zero* (2017), an account of Chekh's service in the army in the war in Donbas, is one of his latest books, for which he became a recipient of several prestigious awards in Ukraine, such as the Joseph Conrad Prize (2019), the Gogol Prize (2018), the Voyin Svitla (2018), and the Litaktsent Prize (2017). This is his first book-length translation into English.

Buy it > www.glagoslav.com

THE VILLAGE TEACHER AND OTHER STORIES
by Theodore Odrach

The twenty-two stories in this collection, set mostly in Eastern Europe during World War Two, depict a world fraught with conflict and chaos. Theodore Odrach is witness to the horrors that surround him, and as both an investigative journalist and a skilful storyteller, using humor and irony, he guides us through his remarkable narratives. His writing style is clean and spare, yet at the same time compelling and complex. There is no short supply of triumph and catastrophe, courage and cowardice, good and evil, as they impact the lives of ordinary people.

In "Benny's Story", a group of prisoners fight to survive despite horrific circumstances; in "Lickspittles", the absurdity of an émigré writer's life is highlighted; in "Blood", a young man travels to a distant city in search of his lost love; in "Whistle Stop", two German soldiers fight boredom in an out-of-the-way outpost, only to see their world crumble and fall.

Buy it > www.glagoslav.com

Glagoslav Publications Catalogue

- *The Time of Women* by Elena Chizhova
- *Andrei Tarkovsky: A Life on the Cross* by Lyudmila Boyadzhieva
- *Sin* by Zakhar Prilepin
- *Hardly Ever Otherwise* by Maria Matios
- *Khatyn* by Ales Adamovich
- *The Lost Button* by Irene Rozdobudko
- *Christened with Crosses* by Eduard Kochergin
- *The Vital Needs of the Dead* by Igor Sakhnovsky
- *The Sarabande of Sara's Band* by Larysa Denysenko
- *A Poet and Bin Laden* by Hamid Ismailov
- *Zo Gaat Dat in Rusland* (Dutch Edition) by Maria Konjoekova
- *Kobzar* by Taras Shevchenko
- *The Stone Bridge* by Alexander Terekhov
- *Moryak* by Lee Mandel
- *King Stakh's Wild Hunt* by Uladzimir Karatkevich
- *The Hawks of Peace* by Dmitry Rogozin
- *Harlequin's Costume* by Leonid Yuzefovich
- *Depeche Mode* by Serhii Zhadan
- *Groot Slem en Andere Verhalen* (Dutch Edition) by Leonid Andrejev
- *METRO 2033* (Dutch Edition) by Dmitry Glukhovsky
- *METRO 2034* (Dutch Edition) by Dmitry Glukhovsky
- *A Russian Story* by Eugenia Kononenko
- *Herstories, An Anthology of New Ukrainian Women Prose Writers*
- *The Battle of the Sexes Russian Style* by Nadezhda Ptushkina
- *A Book Without Photographs* by Sergey Shargunov
- *Down Among The Fishes* by Natalka Babina
- *disUNITY* by Anatoly Kudryavitsky
- *Sankya* by Zakhar Prilepin
- *Wolf Messing* by Tatiana Lungin
- *Good Stalin* by Victor Erofeyev
- *Solar Plexus* by Rustam Ibragimbekov
- *Don't Call me a Victim!* by Dina Yafasova
- *Poetin* (Dutch Edition) by Chris Hutchins and Alexander Korobko

- *A History of Belarus* by Lubov Bazan
- *Children's Fashion of the Russian Empire* by Alexander Vasiliev
- *Empire of Corruption: The Russian National Pastime* by Vladimir Soloviev
- *Heroes of the 90s: People and Money. The Modern History of Russian Capitalism* by Alexander Solovev, Vladislav Dorofeev and Valeria Bashkirova
- *Fifty Highlights from the Russian Literature* (Dutch Edition) by Maarten Tengbergen
- *Bajesvolk* (Dutch Edition) by Michail Chodorkovsky
- *Dagboek van Keizerin Alexandra* (Dutch Edition)
- *Myths about Russia* by Vladimir Medinskiy
- *Boris Yeltsin: The Decade that Shook the World* by Boris Minaev
- *A Man Of Change: A study of the political life of Boris Yeltsin*
- *Sberbank: The Rebirth of Russia's Financial Giant* by Evgeny Karasyuk
- *To Get Ukraine* by Oleksandr Shyshko
- *Asystole* by Oleg Pavlov
- *Gnedich* by Maria Rybakova
- *Marina Tsvetaeva: The Essential Poetry*
- *Multiple Personalities* by Tatyana Shcherbina
- *The Investigator* by Margarita Khemlin
- *The Exile* by Zinaida Tulub
- *Leo Tolstoy: Flight from Paradise* by Pavel Basinsky
- *Moscow in the 1930* by Natalia Gromova
- *Laurus* (Dutch edition) by Evgenij Vodolazkin
- *Prisoner* by Anna Nemzer
- *The Crime of Chernobyl: The Nuclear Goulag* by Wladimir Tchertkoff
- *Alpine Ballad* by Vasil Bykau
- *The Complete Correspondence of Hryhory Skovoroda*
- *The Tale of Aypi* by Ak Welsapar
- *Selected Poems* by Lydia Grigorieva
- *The Fantastic Worlds of Yuri Vynnychuk*
- *The Garden of Divine Songs and Collected Poetry of Hryhory Skovoroda*
- *Adventures in the Slavic Kitchen: A Book of Essays with Recipes* by Igor Klekh
- *Seven Signs of the Lion* by Michael M. Naydan

- *Forefathers' Eve* by Adam Mickiewicz
- *One-Two* by Igor Eliseev
- *Girls, be Good* by Bojan Babić
- *Time of the Octopus* by Anatoly Kucherena
- *The Grand Harmony* by Bohdan Ihor Antonych
- *The Selected Lyric Poetry Of Maksym Rylsky*
- *The Shining Light* by Galymkair Mutanov
- *The Frontier: 28 Contemporary Ukrainian Poets - An Anthology*
- *Acropolis: The Wawel Plays* by Stanisław Wyspiański
- *Contours of the City* by Attyla Mohylny
- *Conversations Before Silence: The Selected Poetry of Oles Ilchenko*
- *The Secret History of my Sojourn in Russia* by Jaroslav Hašek
- *Mirror Sand: An Anthology of Russian Short Poems*
- *Maybe We're Leaving* by Jan Balaban
- *Death of the Snake Catcher* by Ak Welsapar
- *A Brown Man in Russia* by Vijay Menon
- *Hard Times* by Ostap Vyshnia
- *The Flying Dutchman* by Anatoly Kudryavitsky
- *Nikolai Gumilev's Africa* by Nikolai Gumilev
- *Combustions* by Srđan Srdić
- *The Sonnets* by Adam Mickiewicz
- *Dramatic Works* by Zygmunt Krasiński
- *Four Plays* by Juliusz Słowacki
- *Little Zinnobers* by Elena Chizhova
- *We Are Building Capitalism! Moscow in Transition 1992-1997* by Robert Stephenson
- *The Nuremberg Trials* by Alexander Zvyagintsev
- *The Hemingway Game* by Evgeni Grishkovets
- *A Flame Out at Sea* by Dmitry Novikov
- *Jesus' Cat* by Grig
- *Want a Baby and Other Plays* by Sergei Tretyakov
- *Mikhail Bulgakov: The Life and Times* by Marietta Chudakova
- *Leonardo's Handwriting* by Dina Rubina
- *A Burglar of the Better Sort* by Tytus Czyżewski
- *The Mouseiad and other Mock Epics* by Ignacy Krasicki
- *Ravens before Noah* by Susanna Harutyunyan

- *An English Queen and Stalingrad* by Natalia Kulishenko
- *Point Zero* by Narek Malian
- *Absolute Zero* by Artem Chekh
- *Olanda* by Rafał Wojasiński
- *Robinsons* by Aram Pachyan
- *The Monastery* by Zakhar Prilepin
- *The Selected Poetry of Bohdan Rubchak: Songs of Love, Songs of Death, Songs of the Moon*
- *Mebet* by Alexander Grigorenko
- *The Orchestra* by Vladimir Gonik
- *Everyday Stories* by Mima Mihajlović
- *Slavdom* by Ľudovít Štúr
- *The Code of Civilization* by Vyacheslav Nikonov
- *Where Was the Angel Going?* by Jan Balaban
- *De Zwarte Kip* (Dutch Edition) by Antoni Pogorelski
- *Głosy / Voices* by Jan Polkowski
- *Sergei Tretyakov: A Revolutionary Writer in Stalin's Russia* by Robert Leach
- *Opstand* (Dutch Edition) by Władysław Reymont
- *Dramatic Works* by Cyprian Kamil Norwid
- *Children's First Book of Chess* by Natalie Shevando and Matthew McMillion
- *Precursor* by Vasyl Shevchuk
- *The Vow: A Requiem for the Fifties* by Jiří Kratochvil
- *De Bibliothecaris* (Dutch edition) by Mikhail Jelizarov
- *Subterranean Fire* by Natalka Bilotserkivets
- *Vladimir Vysotsky: Selected Works*
- *Behind the Silk Curtain* by Gulistan Khamzayeva
- *The Village Teacher and Other Stories* by Theodore Odrach
- *Duel* by Borys Antonenko-Davydovych
- *War Poems* by Alexander Korotko
- *Ballads and Romances* by Adam Mickiewicz
- *The Revolt of the Animals* by Wladyslaw Reymont
- *Liza's Waterfall: The hidden story of a Russian feminist* by Pavel Basinsky
- *Biography of Sergei Prokofiev* by Igor Vishnevetsky

    More coming ...

GLAGOSLAV PUBLICATIONS
www.glagoslav.com